AF526771

Hampi

Hampi

Discover the Splendours of Vijayanagar

SUBHADRA SEN GUPTA

Photographs by

CLARE ARNI

NIYOGI
BOOKS

Published by
NIYOGI BOOKS
Block D, Building No. 77,
Okhla Industrial Area, Phase-I,
New Delhi-110 020, INDIA
Tel: 91-11-26816301, 26818960
Email: niyogibooks@gmail.com
Website: www.niyogibooksindia.com

Text: Subhadra Sen Gupta
Photographs © Clare Arni
Design: Nabanita Das/Niyogi Books
Editor: Madhuparna Banerjee/Niyogi Books

ISBN: 978-81-89738-64-8
Publication: 2010
First reprint: 2016
Second reprint: 2019
Third reprint: 2022

All rights are reserved. No part of this publication may be reproduced or transmitted in any form or by any means, electronic or mechanical, including photocopying, recording or by any information storage and retrieval system without prior written permission and consent of the publisher.

Printed at: Niyogi Offset Pvt. Ltd., New Delhi, India.

Contents

7 Introduction

15 One - **A City Time Forgot**
The landscape and panorama of Hampi today

39 Two - **A Kingdom by the Tungabhadra**
History of the foundation of the Vijayanagar Empire

71 Three - **From Zenith to Oblivion**
History of the greatest years of the Vijayanagar Empire

109 Four - **Krishnadeva Raya**
Profile of the greatest monarch of Vijayanagar

127 Five - **Living in Vijayanagar**
Recreating the life of the people

157 Six - **Pilgrims by a Sacred River**
The art and architecture of the temples of Hampi

203 Seven - **A Quiet Pause at Vitthala**
Experience the ambience at a unique temple

217 Eight - **An Imperial Citadel**
The majestic architecture of the Royal Enclosure

252 Chronology
253 Further Reading
254 Maps
256 Index

Introduction

A visit to Hampi captures the imagination in many vivid ways. Here is the personal response of the writer and photographer of this book to a place they have grown to love.

Listen to a Silent City...

Even for a traveller who has visited many historical sites in South India, Hampi promises a peerless experience. I have wandered through many temple precincts and marvelled at the soaring *gopurams* but Hampi brings in addition, a royal enclave attached to its sacred zone. The grandeur of many royal palaces have filled me with astonishment but they did not possess the spiritual resonance that I sensed at the ancient Virupaksha Temple at Hampi. It is really very difficult for anyone to compare the experience of Hampi with any other place in South India; it is truly, a one of a kind phenomenon.

For me, Hampi is like a palimpsest of the passage of time. This medieval metropolis with a citadel and sacred centre thrived for three hundred years but then in the 16th century it was totally destroyed by Muslim invaders and the city was abandoned. The wood and brick palaces were burnt to ashes, leaving just the stone basements behind, images lay smashed where they fell and pillars crumbled to the ground. What followed over the next four centuries was the gentle but inexorable march of nature across the devastated landscape. Creepers grew across the fallen columns, pipal saplings raised their heads above dilapidated gateways and grass sprouted over broken masonry. The villagers planted rows of paddy around collapsed pavilions and used the exquisitely carved stones to prop up the thatched roofs of their mundane huts. A magnificent metropolis merged back into the landscape and was forgotten by history.

There is just one other medieval Indian city, that I can think of, that has been frozen in the past like this – Akbar's Fatehpur Sikri near Agra. Thinking of Hampi–Vijayanagar and Fatehpur Sikri, I have discovered many similarities between them. Both of them were abandoned in the 16th century and never came to life again. They were imperial capitals of great empires—Vijayanagar and the Mughals. They were also inspired by the spirit of two truly enlightened monarchs—Krishnadeva Raya and Jalaluddin Akbar.

Vijayanagar and Fatehpur Sikri were cities that flourished through trade. The cities were visited by travellers from across the world who were dazzled by their magnificence and left memoirs capturing their vivid life. Lively, gossipy chronicles of prosperous bazaars; busy inns; musicians, dancers and poets, all patronised by a generous nobility. Most importantly, their societies were remarkably tolerant in an intolerant medieval world. Akbar married Hindu princesses, had Hindu ministers and generals and got the Mahabharata translated into Persian. Krishnadeva Raya had whole battalions of Muslim soldiers who were allowed to take their oath of allegiance on the Koran. When Krishnadeva sat in court both the Hindu scriptures and the Koran were kept beside him and after successful military campaigns he honoured Hindu, Muslim and Portuguese generals.

Both the cities are the anti-thesis of our image of medieval societies. They were open to the world. Where Vijayanagar triumphs is in its respect for women. None of the contemporary chroniclers mention purdah in the kingdom. Women were educated and one traveller mentions numerous girls' schools. Another tells us that women were employed in the royal establishment not just as maids, cooks or companions, but also as administrators and accountants. Some women even became wrestlers!

So during your visit to Hampi a little knowledge of its history would help. This book has two chapters that encapsulate the main stream of events from the foundation of the empire to its oblivion. Chapter 3 gives the history of the period when Vijayanagar was at its zenith and a quick read of it will help you appreciate what you see around you. The following chapters give detailed information about all the important monuments that are worth visiting.

To truly savour a place like Hampi you have to alert all your senses. It is not just a visual but a completely tactile experience of touch, smell, sound, and a combination of landscape and architecture. There are the ochre stone hills framing the grey green waters of the Tungabhadra that shimmer in the early morning light. The sunlight is a haze of gold that creeps into abandoned temples through chinks in the walls and falls at the feet of a goddess like a devoted penitent.

As you wander through the *mandapa* of a silent temple, take off your shoes and feel the cool stone under your feet. Touch a pillar and follow the lines of carvings of a dancing Shiva and you'll be able to imagine what that forgotten stone carver felt as he tapped the unyielding stone with his chisel. Listen to the silence as you watch the sun dip past the gigantic head of the Narasimha statue that still watches over Hampi with such ferocious pride.

For the devout, the living shrine of Virupaksha beckons and so do small wayside temples and monastic retreats. If you take an early morning walk by the Hemkuta Hill you'll hear the atonal chanting of Vedic mantras in the temple of Saint Vidyaranya, interspersed by the flutter of pigeons' wings and the shrill calls of eagles. Time stands still at such moments and Hampi becomes a part of your imagination for ever.

For me the most haunting place in Hampi is the long stretch of abandoned arcades they call Hampi Bazaar. At one end is the boulder strewn slope of the Matanga Hill and at the other the first *gopuram* of the Virupaksha Temple. Connecting the two is the broad avenue with rows of rooms on both sides, a colonnade that must have housed shops. This is the road that all travellers describe with wonder, a bazaar that sold everything from silks, gold and diamonds to flowers, spices and betel leaf. Here courtesans danced before the festival chariot of the deities as the air reverberated to flutes and drums and elephants and horses paraded by. Hampi Bazaar is where the spiritual and sacred met the temporal and royal, as kings bowed before the eternal power of the true monarchs of Vijayanagar—Lord Shiva–Virupaksha and his consort, the Devi Parvati–Pampa. Take a moment on a quiet afternoon, sit inside one of the empty cubicles, lean against a cool pillar and let your imagination fill the avenue with pageantry from the past and you'll sense why Hampi is so special.

As you stand on top of the Mahanavami platform and look around the desolate landscape, compare it to the busy courtyards of the Virupaksha Temple. I was once on top of the platform at sunset and as the light darkened, all around me were ruins—broken patches of tilting walls, the stark span of the platforms over which once the beautiful palaces had stood and bits of carved stone sticking out of the ground that no one can identify any longer. A place that was once the kaleidoscopic heart of an empire reverberating to pomp and pageantry, turned into a landscape blasted by the destructive force of envy and malice.

In contrast, the precincts of the Virupaksha Temple are full of all the joys of life, busy with priests and pilgrims. Watch the dark eyes of children running about and the bright saris of the women gleaming against the white dhotis of the men, as the air echoes to the continuous clanging of bells and voices chanting prayers. Take a happy sniff of the aroma of incense smoke and flowers and you realise that at Hampi the temporal world of kings and queens may have vanished but the sacred empire of the gods remains eternal.

Oddly enough it is the same at Fatehpur Sikri, where Akbar's empty palaces loom over echoing courtyards where tourists wander during the day time but as dusk falls, it all turns eerily silent and the ghosts flit by to a forgotten jangle of anklets. Right next to the citadel is the mosque and the shrine of the Sufi saint Sheikh Salim Chishti and here pilgrims from every faith come to pray, as they have done for six centuries and at the door of the dargah, qawwali singers raise their voices in prayer. In India the royal panoply of power is always transient, what stays engraved in the hearts of the people are the sanctuaries of the holy.

Hampi means different things to different people. For the artistic imagination it is like a living gallery of sculpture and architecture and for the historian a perfectly preserved page from the past. For the curious traveller it is a journey into another time and for the pilgrim a moment of solace and peace. Whatever you may seek in unforgettable Hampi–Vijayanagar, I promise you, you will not be disappointed.

Once you have seen this city petrified in stone you will never forget it. Let Hampi take you over, surrender to its magic and listen to its quiet, wise voice. It will change you for ever.

–Subhadra Sen Gupta

A Place of the Imagination...

Hampi is interesting, not just as a dry as dust academic site, but an exciting and ever-changing place that exists as much in the present as it does in the past. Alongside the ancient ruins and prehistoric rocks thrives a population and a culture that is still evolving so that when I walk the streets of Hampi Bazaar or the Royal Enclosure, the feeling in the air is not one of decline but one of renewal.

The colours, smells and sounds, the vibrancy and the urgency in the air makes the Vijayanagar site a special place for those interested in humanity, rather than history. Here hereditary priests, ascetics and sadhus mix with foreign tourists, trance music reverberates across the three hundred-year-old buildings of the Hampi Bazaar and where those that seek enlightenment live in caves and bathe in the Tungabhadra River. Even in the deserted ruins, the rubble and the remains are populated by characters from one's mind, since Hampi is, above all, a place of the imagination.

The first place a visitor comes to is Hampi Bazaar—the main marketplace and the thumping commercial heart of Vijayanagar. It is a long, wide street, bordered by stone colonnades, where the shopkeepers and artisans would have produced and sold their wares. At one end is the ivory-white *gopuram* of the main Virupaksha Temple and at the other end rises the stone steps of Matanga Hill. The Bazaar is bustling, filled with traders, tourists, pilgrims, saffron-clad sadhus, policemen, cows and every form of life that an Indian market can produce. The smell of bananas, goats, hot chai and fried food fills the air and grows stronger. This is Hampi's living past, people worshipping at a site that has been a source of pilgrimage for hundreds of years.

In other parts of Hampi, the crowds and bustle are confined to the imagination. In the Queen's Bathing Pool, perhaps certain views were always strictly imaginary, but the echoes of laughter and the chatter and the sights of saris drying in the sun still remain in this arched and delicately stuccoed building. The courtyard, open to the sky, is profoundly evocative with its tank and many pillared halls that still echo with the sounds of water and laughter, despite being long dry and embellished by generations of amorous graffiti.

Wandering through Hampi, there is an abundance of individual images and impressions that stand out—the long row of enormous arches of the Elephant Stables, capped with their elegant domes, the beautiful and seemingly interleaved columns and pillars of the Lotus Mahal, the solitary sentry tower standing guard for centuries. Every scene and sight in Hampi seems to have been deliberately composed with a sophisticated and painterly eye, as great boulders, startling green paddy fields and stone temples complement each other and are therefore, a photographer's dream.

Hampi is also full of hidden things. Just beyond the Bazaar there is a wonderful walk to Kotalingam where *lingam*s are carved straight on to the living rocks. It is thrilling to discover them as you wander between the boulders (and occasionally leap from one to another) to find these sculptures seemingly placed at random amongst the serene landscape. From Kotalingam you can see the slow-flowing Tungabhadra meander past you, dotted with coracles, and beyond it a great hill of broken boulders rises into the air. Among the natural shapes are more deliberate ones—temples, stairways, a Nandi bull, the strange, discordant remains of the Vijayanagar civilisation.

Getting to know Hampi is a complex and very personal journey; it is a place to visit and revisit. You slowly become attached to favourite places, dismiss others as mere tourist spots, get to know the characters that fill the scenes and begin to claim some aspect or understanding of the place as entirely your own. Places like Kotalingam where the nature of your first discovery and your subsequently evolving encounters result in a relationship as subtle as one that you can have with an individual. You witness sights that are so ephemeral that you feel yourself privileged to have seen that particular aspect of Hampi. A majestic sunset is watched every evening by rows of langur monkeys, sitting high among the rocks, doing nothing but watching darkness fall. A coracle, hopelessly over-stuffed, disgorges goats, a motorbike, two bicycles and a few ruffled tourists on to the stone embankment. A pale sadhu comes down to bathe in the twilight, chanting in a low reverberating voice.

It is strange that some of the most evocative ruins are the ones that are the least substantial. As less of the structure remains, it is left entirely to the imagination to conjure up most of the structure and the people and movements that attended to it. One such structure is the Mahanavami platform, which was once a hundred-pillared audience hall in the midst of the Royal Enclosure. Now only the substructure remains, the rest was devastated by vengeful invading kingdoms. Yet, as you walk across the summit of this still substantial edifice, decorated with beautiful stone carvings of elephants and hunting scenes, and you look across the ruined city and to the hills beyond, you know that you are walking in the footsteps of ancient kings and the true majesty of Hampi becomes apparent.

The architecture of the Royal Enclosure is still magnificent. The long Elephant Stable (so wide, that it is nearly impossible to get the whole structure in one photograph) is a masterpiece, with great stone fluted arches and capped domes, niches and brickwork in the Bahmani style and it stands as a powerful symbol of the riches of the royalty of Vijayanagar. The Lotus Mahal, a mind-bending structure of seemingly interleaved and interwoven fluted arches and columns, is still standing almost perfectly, its form still conveying the shape of that flower.

From the Mahanavami platform it is not a long walk to a recently discovered treasure. A deep and wide tank is dug straight into the earth. The steps and platforms ranged around the sides form beautiful geometric patterns. You begin to smell the dampness long before you even get to the tank, an evocative aroma amongst the dusty dryness of the site. It was found when the archaeological department uncovered some water channels and decided to find out where they led to. It is evidence of the advanced engineering ability of the kingdom (which was a parallel to the hydraulic achievements of Rome) which they married so well with a profound architectural style to create the monuments of Hampi. It is also evidence, I think, that much more is still to be discovered under the rocks and earth of Hampi and that the site remains a place of hidden treasures.

Hampi is a serene and spiritual place for most of its visitors, but no description of a place is complete without a mention of its conflicts. There are of course many. The desire for better access has been squashed by those interested in conservation. The once majestic Tungabhadra River is greatly reduced by a dam, though most local houses get no running water and very little electricity. Those who wanted to keep the area pure have already been frustrated by the great clutter of wires and lights to satisfy the local government's penchant for 'sound and light' shows. Clumsy cement restorations and heavily watered lawns have lent some areas a somewhat surreal air. Sometimes I fear that Hampi will turn into 'Hampi: The Theme Park', a fear given more credence by the present government's plan to make such a theme park on local university land.

–Abhimanyu and Clare Arni

Chapter One

A CITY TIME FORGOT

The landscape and panorama of Hampi today

Never perhaps in the history of the world has such havoc been wrought, and wrought suddenly, on so splendid a city, teeming with a wealthy and industrious population in the full plenitude of prosperity one day, and on the next seized, pillaged, and reduced to ruins, amid scenes of savage massacre and horrors begging description.

– Robert Sewell, *A Forgotten Empire*

1

It is a landscape that startles you with its sudden changes. As you move south of the mountain ranges of the Vindhyas, it begins with the fertile, verdant green paddy fields along the plains of the Krishna River and then, in the blink of an eye, it transforms itself into a barren, stony, forbidding world beside the mighty waters of the Tungabhadra River. This is an ancient land – of myths of beautiful river goddesses and monkey kings, legends of saints and warriors, and the desolate ruins of a city that vanished from memory.

Pampakshetra – Virupakshapura – Kishkindhakshetra – Bidjanagar – Bisnaga – Vijayanagar. And today, a village called Hampi.

Moving south of the Krishna River, the bumpy road meanders over silver blue canals and dips past banks of betel palms. The land flattens into stretches painted in many shades of green. The paddy fields are expanses of fertile emerald; in the patches growing lentils the green is touched by yellow and then there are the dusty leaf-green bushes of chillies dotted with red. These are interspersed by banana groves where the leaves droop like elephant ears and the tiny golden bunches of fruit hang enticingly below. Along the side

Such wandering mendicants dressed as Lord Shiva have always been seen in sacred Pampakshetra.

Facing page: *A coracle, still a common form of transport in Karnataka, makes its way across the Tungabhadra River.*

Nature's sculptures in granite that frame Hampi's landscape in red-gold majesty.

Pages 14–15: *The Tiruvengalanatha Temple nestles between the boulders of the eastern base of Matanga Hill.*

of the fields, the tall, elegant coconut palms march along in neat military rows.

The ebony-skinned, bare-bodied men clad in gleaming white dhotis and scraps of cloth wrapped around their heads, labour among the rice and lentil crops. The women pick the chillies that they drop into a pouch they make in front using their vividly coloured saris. You are watching them grow their daily meal of rice and *sambar* fiery with chillies, spicy raw banana fry and coconut chutney.

Soon this portrait of a generous, fecund earth changes as along the horizon the first russet-brown boulders appear, looming on top of low hills, tilting precariously along the slopes and lying in a pile at the bottom. It is as if a mythical giant had been at play with the granite stones, piling them up into teetering hills and then throwing them down again. As historian George Michell writes, 'Its unique rocky appearance (is) caused not by earthquake and upheaval but by some

three thousand millions years of erosion.' These granite ranges one day provided the building material for the sumptuous palaces, temples, carved images and miles and miles of the encircling walls of Vijayanagar. The earth turns reddish brown and barren, with patches of scrub and spindly trees. Suddenly the fertile river delta is transformed into a moonscape through which the grey green waters of the Tungabhadra River flow in and out – curving around hills, cascading nonchalantly over chunks of granite, forming lagoons and rocky pools.

In this daunting terrain rose one of the most opulent of medieval cities—Vijayanagar, the City of Victory—a metropolis of rich and busy bazaars, luxurious palaces and fabulous temples. Its skyline was pierced by the soaring *gopurams* of the temple gateways, and Portuguese, Chinese, Malay and Arab travellers wandered around its legendary market streets, marvelling at its glittering shops. Vijayanagar rose to power in the 14th century and was the only Hindu kingdom in the South and its architecture, in the words of the historian Percy Brown, 'represents the supremely passionate flowering of the Dravidian style'. Today Hampi is a World Cultural Heritage Site selected by UNESCO.

Just as its rise and prosperity was the envy of the world, the tragedy of its downfall still permeates the air around the deserted pavilions, smashed pillars and broken images. Once Vijayanagar

A banana plantation creates a patch of mellow, fertile green in the shadows of a hill.

Top: *For a century these stone walls pierced by bastions protected Vijayanagar from invaders.*

fell, it never rose again. Abandoned by its people, it lay in the shadows of history till discovered again in the late 19th century. Today only the tiny village of Hampi survives and all around its red-tile-roofed huts the ruins of Vijayanagar lie scattered – temples, palaces, bazaars, watchtowers, acqueducts, bathing pools, collapsing gateways and walls – an array of beautiful ghosts reminding us of a great empire.

No one forgets the first sight of Hampi. The road from the town of Hospet to Hampi climbs up a hill, curving higher and higher and then there is a steep suicidal turn and your heart stops. Before your eyes is a panorama that can rival anything, anywhere in the world. Spread across the landscape, as far as the eye can see are the remains of a city. Between the stony hills and by the Tungabhadra River and all around Hampi, history awaits you in red-gold silence, frozen in stone.

Meandering granite stairways, an architectural marvel encircle the Matanga Hill.

A River Goddess Named Pampa...

Modern Hampi is a small village (latitude 15 degrees 20′ North and longitude 76 degrees 30′ East) on the southern bank of the Tungabhadra River in the Hospet *taluk* of the Bellary District, Karnataka. The ruins of ancient Vijayanagar are spread over an area of twenty-six kilometres and include several modern villages. Here the Tungabhadra flows north-east in a series of cascades and rapids, and near the city it flows into a narrow gorge surrounded by low hills of boulders – a circle of hills that provide a natural protection from invasions. Among the peaks are the Matanga and Hemkuta at the two ends of the Hampi Bazaar and the Anjenadri and Malayavanta beyond.

The name Hampi is the anglicised version of the Kannada name 'Hampe' which is a mutilated form of the word Pampa. And Hampi traces its beginnings to the times of myths and epics. In ancient Sanskrit and Tamil texts, it is referred to as Pampakshetra and Virupakshapura. Legend connects it to Kishkindha of the epic tale of the Ramayana, the kingdom of the Vanars.

The myths are found in the *sthalapurana* of the Virupaksha Temple. In Hinduism, a *sthalapurana* is the religious history of a pilgrimage or a temple. Pampa is another name of the Tungabhadra River and Pampa Devi was the goddess of the river and a daughter of Lord Brahma. She was determined to marry Lord Shiva and performed years of severe penance to win him. He arrived here in the form of Lord Virupaksha, the 'God with the Oblique Eyes', and showered gold over the Hemkuta Hills in joy. Their celestial marriage is still celebrated every year during the Brahmotsavam festival. So this temple and the village of Hampi predate the Vijayanagar Empire. The temple became the heart of the new city and Lord Virupaksha became the titular deity of the royal family. One day, the greatest king of Vijayanagar, Krishnadeva Raya, would build the soaring *gopuram* that now dominates the landscape.

The Hampi region is also the Kishkindha of the Ramayana, the domain of the monkeys, which was the kingdom of the Vanar kings Valli and Sugriva. Valli had dethroned Sugriva who had

The Vitthala Temple, though no longer a functioning shrine, continuously attracts a multitude of tourists.

taken refuge in the caves of the Matanga Hill with his companion Hanuman. At this time Ravana, the king of Lanka, abducted Sita, the wife of Prince Ram of Ayodhya and on his way back swept over Kishkindha in his flying chariot. A desperate Sita threw out her jewellery which Hanuman collected and showed to Ram when he came searching for her. Ram killed Valli here and crowned Sugriva as king at the site where the Kodandarama Temple now stands. Then Hanuman went off in search of Sita while Ram and Lakshman waited for him at Hampi.

Everywhere are landmarks of that epic story—the Raghunath Temple on Malayavanta Hill where Ram stayed during the monsoon before invading Lanka; a cave behind the Vitthala Temple where Sugriva and Hanuman hid Sita's jewellery; the spot where Valli was cremated after being killed by Ram and a pool named after Sita. The royal chapel is called the Hazara Rama Temple where the walls are covered in carvings depicting the various episodes from the Ramayana. And everywhere on the walls of temples and palaces is the image of Hanuman in profile, with his tail curling up above him to remind us of that immortal story.

An open pillared pavilion amidst hillocks of ochre-coloured boulders.

A fragment of the stone walls that once encircled Vijayanagar, near the Royal Enclosure.

Before Vijayanagar...

This region has been inhabited from the Neolithic times; handmade pottery and ancient drawings on the walls of the caves near the Vitthala Temple prove it. The edicts of King Ashoka of the Maurya Dynasty dating back to the 2nd century BC have been found near Bellary. As many inscriptions prove, the region was part of the kingdoms of the southern dynasties of the Chalukyas, Rashtrakutas, Hoysalas and Yadavas. The local feudatories were often based in the fortress of Anegondi whose hoary walls still stand beside the Tungabhadra. Just before the foundation of Vijayanagar, this region was under the rule of the chieftains of Kampili.

By the 14th century many upheavals had transformed life and polity in North India. The Muslim invaders had conquered the northern region in the last decades of the 12th century and a series

Hampi invites pilgrims to become one with its landscape; they bathe and rest here under the sheltering sky.

of dynasties occupied the throne of Delhi. It was during the reign of Allauddin Khalji that the first serious Muslim incursion was made into the Deccan and it was followed by the armies of Muhammad bin Tughlak. Vijayanagar came into existence as a challenge to these northern invasions.

The foundation of this empire was an unusual alliance between the political ambitions of two intrepid local chieftains, the brothers Harihara and Bukka and the Hindu monastery, the Sharada Peetha Math of Sringeri. The beginnings of Vijayanagar lie in the vision of the head of the monastery, Shankaracharya Vidyaranya of Sringeri, who envisaged an empire that would preserve and propagate the ancient Vedic traditions and culture and have the power to withstand the onslaughts of the Sultanate of Delhi. Vijayanagar succeeded in this mission for over two and a half centuries.

Of *Apsaras* and *Yakshis*...

Vijayanagar shows the final evolution of the architecture of the South, especially the temples, and a little knowledge of the traditional architecture of temples would help in appreciating the temples at Hampi. The *shastra*s are ancient Hindu treatises that laid down the rules of correct conduct and practices and they codify not just the rituals of worship but also the architectural layouts of temples and the placing of images. The *Vastupurusha Mandala* or *Vastu Shastra* was codified in the early years of the first millennium and thus temples built across the Indian subcontinent follow a similar architecture plan. The northern style called *nagara* differs in some ways from the more ornate architecture of the southern Dravidian style.

Stone carvers covered Hampi with joyous sculptures. Here a maze in rows of tiny Shivalingams*.*

A temple is a symbol of heaven, *swarga*, which is located around a mythical mountain named Meru in the Himalayas. So the pantheon of Hindu gods and goddesses, the demigods (*yaksha*s and *yakshi*s) the celestial dancers (*apsara*s) and the musicians (*gandharva*s) are all carved on the walls of the Hindu shrines.

The sanctum sanctorum is the *garbha griha* or the womb house and this small, plain, square cella is the heart of a temple. This is where the image of the main deity is placed and is adorned in silks, gold and jewels and loaded with fragrant flowers. The tall oil lamps burn all around and incense wafts lazily in the air that echoes to the ringing of bells and the chanting of mantras. This is the heart of a temple; every path leads to the *garbha griha* and the temple is built all around it.

The *garbha griha* is surrounded by a corridor called the *pradakshina patha* that is used for the circumambulation of the deity. The tower over the sanctum is the *shikhara*. An open pillared hall attached to the sanctum is the *mandapa* where the devotees gather to watch the religious rituals. In larger temples many *mandapa*s are added; the *bhoga mandapa* is where *yagyas* and offerings are made and the pilgrims fed with the sanctified *prasad*. The *natya mandapa* is the dance hall where the temple dancers, the *devadasi*s, performed offering their dance to their Divine Lord.

In the southern temples a smaller, more ornate shrine stands near the *garbha griha*. This is the *amman* temple for the consort of the deity. At the Virupaksha Temple, there are two *amman* shrines for the goddesses Pampa Devi and Bhuvaneshwari. Finally, there is the *kalyana mandapa* where the most colourful annual festival takes place; here the celestial wedding of the deity and his consort takes place during the Brahmotsavam festival. As pilgrims crowd the bazaars outside, the temple chariot carrying the divine couple is joyously pulled along the roads to the sound of the piping of *nadeshwaram*s and the echoing roll of *mridangam*s.

What makes southern temples so eye-catching are the *gopuram*s. These tall, pyramidal gateways set between the outer walls teem with carvings and are often painted in a vivid palette of colours. The larger temples are enclosed within a series of courtyards called *prakara*s and the *gopuram*s are the gateways set into the walls. So you walk under a row of *gopuram*s of gradually diminishing height until you reach the final courtyard where the deity waits for you.

In ancient times, kings built temples in stone and palaces often in brick and wood. That is why the temples of Hampi have

Anantasayana *Vishnu image carved on a stray boulder.*

The colours of the unique landscape of Hampi – red-gold hills, emerald fields and a sparkling river.

survived better than the buildings in the Royal Enclosure. The palaces had carved stone basements over which elaborate wood and brick structures were built. These superstructures were all destroyed when the city was sacked by Muslim invaders in AD 1565 and all that remains are the stone platforms and a few carved elephant balustrades. A few buildings have remained intact like one palace in the harem called Lotus Mahal, an elephant stable, some military structures like gateways, walls and bastions, and a royal bath house.

Arriving at Bisnaga...

In AD 1897, a Portuguese scholar named Senhor David Lopes discovered an ancient manuscript at the Bibliotheque Nationale in Paris. Written in elaborate calligraphy, the title page read – *Chronica dos reis de Bisnaga,* and it seemed to be reports from two Portuguese travellers in the 16th century to a magnificent South Indian kingdom and its capital city that they called Bisnaga. The two travellers were Fernao Nuniz and Domingo Paes and they were probably writing to a well-known Portuguese historian named Barros in Lisbon.

David Lopes wrote about the chronicles of Paes and Nuniz and published it in Lisbon and then they were translated into English by Robert Sewell in AD 1900 and published as *A Forgotten Empire.*

The sources of the history of Vijayanagar are gleaned from the writings of not just Paes and Nuniz but also a number of other travellers who left behind their travelogues. Another source of history is the hundreds of inscriptions we can still see on the walls of palaces and temples in the region while Pampakshetra and Vijayanagar are often mentioned in contemporary literature in Kannada, Telugu and Tamil.

Travellers and traders came from many countries. Among those who wrote about their experiences was Nicolo dei Conti of Portugal who came in AD 1420 during the reign of Devaraya I. Another Italian, Ludovico di Varthema arrived in AD 1504 and was in the city during the reign of Krishnadeva Raya. Ceasaro Federici in AD 1567 came just after the Battle of Talikota and gives us a first-hand report of the terrible devastation that followed. The Persian, Abdur Razzaq from the court of King Shahrukh of Herat, grandson of Timur, arrived in AD 1422 during the reign of Devaraya II. Most

Sadhus find lonely spots among the hills and caves for their meditation.

of the Portuguese came from Goa—Fernao Nuniz in AD 1535, Domingo Paes in AD 1520, Duarte Barbosa in AD 1501 and also Tome Pires sometime in the 16th century. Even a Russian adventurer, Athanasius Nikitin, has left behind an account of Vijayanagar. Vijayanagar was a truly cosmopolitan city with Portuguese, Italians, Persians, Russians and even Chinese and Arabs wandering around its streets.

They called the city by many distorted and confusing names—Bizenegelia, Bidjanagar, Bisnaga, Bisinega, Bisinegar … . The earliest chronicle is by Nicolo dei Conti, who arrived in the city just after the accession of Devaraya I and later dictated his memoirs to a secretary of the Pope. He describes what was probably the chariot festival, the Brahmotsavam at the Virupaksha Temple and writes, '… at a certain time of the year, their idol is carried through the city, placed between two chariots, in which are young women richly adorned, who sing hymns to the god and accompanied by a great concourse of people.'

As these are the views of a visitor, these chronicles give us rather an original point of view of not just the king and his city but also the lives of ordinary people. As Duarte Barbosa writes, 'The ... houses are thatched, but nonetheless are very well built and arranged according to occupation, in long streets with many open spaces. And the folk here are ever in such numbers that the streets and places cannot contain them.' Then there is an astonished Domingo Paes reporting on the jewellery worn by the *devadasi*s of Vijayanagar dancing before the king during the Mahanavami festival, 'Who can fitly describe to you the great riches these women carry on their person?... collars of gold with so many diamonds, rubies and pearls, bracelets also on their arms and on their upper arms, girdles below, and of necessity anklets on their feet.'

Pilgrims dry their clothes in the busy Virupaksha Temple courtyard.

Facing page: *Ancient waterworks and canals still irrigate the coconut and banana plantations beside the Tiruvengalanatha Temple.*

These boulders, precariously balanced on top of a hill, create nature's very own art gallery.

Hampi Revived...

The Vijayanagar Empire was destroyed when the combined armies of the neighbouring Muslims kingdoms defeated Vijayanagar in AD 1565. The city was occupied, the temples hammered to the ground, the images of the deities shattered, palaces set on fire and the city abandoned by its people. Most of the deities in the temples were destroyed so that today their *garbha griha*s lie empty, dark and eerily silent. After a while, all that remained were the tiny villages of Hampi and Kamalapuram. Kingdoms rose and fell all around it and Vijayanagar and its magnificent history entered the realm of legends and mythical stories.

Through the relentless depredations of time many of the buildings collapsed, creepers grew out of the ceilings and lintels and

A pillared pavilion that may have been a lookout point, stands on top of a hill above Hampi.

water tanks were covered in silt or buried underground. The farmers planted paddy around the palaces, they built huts using broken pillars and the women dried their saris over the ancient walls. Vijayanagar merged back into the eternal rural landscape, withdrawing into silence and solitude and the only life to be seen here was the ebb and flow of pilgrims around the ruined bazaar leading to the Virupaksha Temple.

It was in the 19th century that this region became a part of the British Empire and English magistrates and engineers rediscovered the ruins. In the late 19th century, Robert Sewell, a member of the Indian Civil Service, discovered the memoirs of two medieval Portuguese travellers Fernao Nuniz and Domingo Paes and painstakingly gathered together the history of Vijayanagar. After his book *A Forgotten Empire* was published in 1900, Hampi was once again to be found on the itineraries of historians and archaeologists.

Once discovered, magnificent Hampi-Vijayanagar will never be forgotten again.

SPELLING PUZZLES

Writers in medieval times were not too particular about spellings and for a European traveller Indian names were both difficult to spell and to remember. So while reading the chronicles of the various travellers to Vijayanagar, one is confronted by a puzzling selection of spellings that are at times quite difficult to decipher.

Take the name of the kingdom. Vijayanagar is spelled as Bisnaga, Bichenagar, Bidjanagar, Bisnagar, Bizenegalia, Visajanagar and Beejanugger. Among the names of the various kings it is easy to understand that Deorao refers to Deva Raya and Bucarao to Bukka Raya but when Harihara is referred to as Pureoyre Deo, it is much harder to sort out.

Then the Islamic names seemed to completely defeat the Europeans. For instance, Togao Mamede refers to Mohammad Tughlaq. Ydallcao to Adil Khan of Bijapur and Ozemelluco was the Nizam-ul-Mulk. For some reason the title Malik Naib led to something close to pure gibberish—Melliquiniby, Enybiquemelly and Melinebique!

Names of places provided another challenge and one has to admit that the writers did create some real tongue-twisters. So Charamoadell referred to Cholamandalam; Cenderghiria to Chandragiri; Odeschiria was Udayagiri; Mamgalor was of course Mangalore and Nagumdym was Anegondi. Then they often refer to Vijayanagar as the 'Kingdom of Narsymga' or Narasimha.

HAMPI MUSEUM

Hampi is a UNESCO World Cultural Heritage Site. The Archaeological Survey of India Museum is located at Kamalapuram. It is worth a visit as it has an excellent collection of sculptures, jewellery, weapons and manuscripts. Also in the courtyard there is a scale model of Hampi that provides a fascinating panorama of the whole area.

Timing: 10 a.m. to 5 p.m. (Closed on Friday).

FESTIVALS

Virupaksha Car Festival. The chariot festival at the Virupaksha Temple. March–April.

Purandara Dasa Music Festival – January–February.

Vijayanagar Cultural Festival – December.

GETTING THERE

By Air: Nearest airports – Bellary (74 km), Belgaum (190 km), Bangalore (353 km), Goa (323 km).

By Rail: Nearest railway station – Hospet (13 km). Hospet is connected to Bangalore by overnight train.

By Road: Daily buses from Bangalore to Hospet. From Hospet to Hampi – buses, auto-rickshaws and cars are available.

Best time to visit: October–March.

Chapter Two

A KINGDOM BY THE TUNGABHADRA

History of the foundation of the Vijayanagar Empire

Protection of dharma was the avowed purpose for which the heroic Sangama brothers founded the new kingdom. The rulers pursued a deliberate policy of tolerance towards followers of all faiths, not excluding the Muslims. The innumerable shrines and temples found all over the capital city – Jaina, Shaiva, Vaishnava and Sakta – and the Muslim quarters … are eloquent witness to this policy.

– S Srinivasachar

2

The story of Vijayanagar really begins in AD 1294, four decades before the foundation of the kingdom, in a tiny fiefdom of North India called Kara. It was a part of the kingdom of the Khalji Dynasty that was ruled from its seat in Delhi by Sultan Jalaluddin Khalji. Kara was under the Sultan's nephew, a ruthlessly ambitious Afghan prince named Garshasp Malik.

Sometimes the seeds of greatness have strange, obscure and truly inexplicable beginnings. Vijayanagar's origins can be traced back to the avaricious gleam in Garshasp Malik's eyes, his overweening aspirations, bottomless greed, and intriguingly, his troubled relationship with his imperious wife and interfering mother-in-law.

Looking South...

Sultan Jalaluddin Khalji of Delhi was a gentle, civilised man who was so fond of his nephew that he had married his daughter to him. Unfortunately, the princess was a haughty and disdainful woman who never let her husband forget that she had married beneath herself. And her interfering mother, Jalaluddin's wife Malika Jahan, added her two bits to the spicy domestic brew by constantly

Expressive stone carving of a warrior still stands by a gateway.

Facing page: *The row of pillars once supported a bridge that spanned the Tungabhadra River.*

goading and scheming against her hapless son-in-law. Garshasp, sitting in obscure Kara, far away from the seat of power in Delhi, now eyed the throne and began a carefully planned campaign to seize it.

A supremely pragmatic and pitiless man, Garshasp knew that his first requirement was a lot of money. He had to build up an army to fight the sons of Jalaluddin who were after all the rightful heirs to the throne and had their formidable mother to support them. Then he would also have to bribe the Delhi nobility into submission. This is when his eyes turned to the Hindu kingdoms in the South that were known for their wealth and also had temples loaded with treasures. Garshasp took permission from his uncle for a campaign to Malwa and then turned southward in a clandestine expedition

Pages 38–39: *A group of school girls bathe in the river, adding a splash of vibrant colours to the landscape.*

A wooden temple chariot that is taken out in procession during the Brahmotsavam festival.

seeking plunder. In AD 1294 he attacked the Yadava kingdom of Devagiri in North Deccan ruled by Raja Ramachandra Deva.

This expedition was the first time that any general of the Delhi Sultanate had attacked a southern kingdom. A complacent Ramachandra Deva was surprised and overwhelmed and Devagiri soon admitted defeat. Garshasp who was not interested in conquest, quickly left with whatever he could plunder from the compliant Yadava king and a long camel train wended its way north loaded with treasures—gold, silver, precious gems, silks; and also horses and elephants. In that train of booty there was also a Yadava princess who had been married to the conqueror.

Soon after, Garshasp murdered his trusting and affectionate uncle, foiled an attempt by Malika Jahan to put her son on the

The steps at the end of the Bazaar, lead tourists to spectacular walks up the Matanga Hill.

Carving of Lord Hanuman in the Guard's Quarters below a gateway.

throne and usurped the Sultanate. Once in power at Delhi he used his newly won southern wealth to bribe the nobility into compliance. As a contemporary historian wrote cynically, the new Sultan won over the nobles with, 'a lavish distribution of Deccan gold'.

Garshasp Malik now took the title of Allauddin Khalji and it was he who began the tradition of regular southern expeditions purely in search of plunder but as always, religion was going to cover a multitude of sins. Now the armies of the Delhi sultans would regularly head south of the Vindhyas wearing the garb of the holy warriors of Islam. There had been Muslim sultans ruling from Delhi for a century but none of them had ventured South before. Allauddin can take the credit for starting this history of pillage and destruction that would one day lead to the rise of the last great Hindu kingdom of the land that resisted this relentless tide for two and a half centuries – magnificent and unforgettable Vijayanagar.

The Khaljis and Tughlaks were never interested in annexing the region – it was too far and too difficult to control. All they wanted was that the southern kings as docile vassals keep sending generous tributes. The system was simple – whenever any king failed to deliver, the armies of Delhi would sweep down to kill, destroy and plunder with vicious abandon. After decades of such attacks, the older kingdoms became so weakened that their decline in fact helped the rise of Vijayanagar as the new, vigorous power that gradually annexed most of modern Karnataka, Tamil Nadu, Kerala and parts of Andhra Pradesh and Maharashtra.

Vijayanagar became the final frontier against the Muslim onslaught and played a crucial role in preserving the ancient Indian culture, not just in architecture and sculpture but also actively patronised literature, religious studies, music and dance. From 12th century onwards, the old Brahmanical heritage had been battered in the North by iconoclastic invaders like Mahmud of Ghazni and Timur. As always, their real purpose was to loot the wealthy temples but they also destroyed and pillaged in the name of Islam. Then followed centuries of Muslim rule where kings claimed the title of Ghazi and took credit for destroying temples and monasteries.

To give an example, the city of Varanasi has a history lost in the hoary mists of time. It is the oldest city in the land but today it has no surviving monument that can be dated beyond the 18th century. And this was a city where 2,500 years ago, the Buddha had walked by the ghats of the Ganga and visited its temples to hold religious debates with Brahmin scholars. Once the land was dotted with Buddhist stupas and viharas and there were great centres of learning in Nalanda, Taxila and Sarnath but most of them have vanished. In some ways, Buddhism suffered more from the invasions as the religion was completely obliterated from the land of its origins and people even forgot that Gautama Buddha was born in the Indian subcontinent.

If today South India still has such magnificent Hindu architecture and an unbroken tradition of cultural and religious life it is because the enlightened kings of Vijayanagar repaired and built temples all across South India and were active in their encouragement of sculptors, poets, singers and dancers. As a matter of fact, the

The gopuram *of the Virupaksha Temple looms over Hampi.*

royal family took great pride in their literary abilities and one of Krishnadeva Raya's compositions, a long poem called *Amulyamalyada* has survived till today.

Generations of kings built a magnificent city, filling it with gigantic palaces and temples with soaring *gopuram* gateways, elegant pavilions, long vistas of bazaars and delicately sculpted water pools. Even today as you wander through the ruined avenues, sit by the empty arcades and peep into dark, silent temples you can sense its lost majesty. These unforgettable ruins still carry an echo of Vijayanagar's many-hued culture, generosity of spirit and open, welcoming tolerance.

A view of the Hampi Bazaar street from the base of Matanga Hill.

Southern Kingdoms...

When the 14th century dawned, the political map of South India was a crazy quilt of ancient kingdoms and powerful principalities that rose and fell with profligate abandon. North Deccan had the Yadava kingdom of Devagiri; then came the Kakatiya kings based at the mud fortress of Warangal; the Hoysalas who built the exquisite Belur and Halebid temples ruled from Dvarasamudra, the Gajapati kings of Kalinga controlled the region of modern Orissa and at the southernmost tip of the peninsula was the kingdom of the Pandyas of Ma'bar. There was no peace among them and they were always waiting for an opportune moment to invade each other's kingdoms. Alliances rose and fell at the whim of kings and even when faced by the marauding armies of the North they never united to face this danger. Alliances were opportunistic and ephemeral, for example, Devagiri became a loyal vassal of the Khaljis and even allowed the Sultan's armies to camp within the kingdom as they marched southwards. In AD 1192, when Muhammad of Ghur had invaded India, the Hindu kingdoms of the North had failed to unite against him and had been obliterated but no lessons had been learnt and the story was going to be repeated in the South.

On his coins Allauddin styled himself as 'the second Alexander' but his biggest military triumphs were really the work of his trusted general Malik Kafur. After Gujarat, Ranthambhor and Mewar fell in the North, the Sultan's armies now turned southwards. As Kafur swept into the Deccan in AD 1300, as always, he had no wish to annex the kingdoms; he only wanted their submission and rich tribute. When he returned after defeating Prataparudra I, the Kakatiya

The village that stands in the shadow of the Virupaksha Temple is the oldest living settlement in Hampi and predates Vijayanagar.

king of Warangal, the historian Amir Khusro writes that the booty moved, 'on a thousand camels groaning under the weight of treasures'. As the most eminent historian of the South, Nilakanta Sastri writes, 'As sultan, Ala-ud-din pursued a policy of plunder and loot in the South in preference to the extension of his territories.'

Kafur was not going to stop. One after another the kings fell before his plundering army – Vir Ballala, the Hoysala king of Dvarasamudra, the Pandyas of Ma'bar – until Kafur reached Rameshwaram at the southernmost tip of the peninsula. After slaughtering thousands, sacking cities and destroying innumerable temples he returned to Delhi in AD 1311 with a vast booty that Muslim historians recorded with glee. He brought back 612 elephants, 20,000 horses, boxes of precious gems and pearls and 96,000 *maunds* of gold.

One day the rising anger of the populace at such wanton violence and pillage would lead the people of the South to support the five sons of Sangama in laying the foundation of a new kingdom they named Vijayanagar. The active help of chieftains and rich merchants of the region played a crucial role in the successful rise and survival of the kingdom.

The Khalji Dynasty faded at the death of Allauddin in AD 1316 to be replaced by the Tughlaks. The period of political confusion in the North allowed the southern kingdoms to recover and re-assert their power. In AD 1312, Ramachandra Deva died and his son Shankara Deva became the king of Devagiri. Unlike his father, he had always been hostile to the Khalji presence in his kingdom and he promptly stopped paying tribute. Kafur descended on Devagiri and after Shankara Deva died fighting, he annexed the kingdom. However, some parts of the kingdom refused to submit and one of them was the tiny principality of Kampili in the region of modern Karnataka.

Kampili proclaimed its independence under a local chieftain named Singeya Nayaka and his kingdom included the present day Bellary, Raichur and Dharwar region. Nayaka's energetic

The Tungabhadra River weaves its way through the Vijayanagar capital.

The mighty gopuram *of the Virupaksha Temple, gleaming in the sun, towers above the surrounding landscape.*

son Kampiladeva then began to extend the borders of the kingdom through conquests and built a series of fortresses. One of them was the fort of Anegondi by the northern banks of the Tungabhadra River. In today's Hampi if you sit on the stone steps of the river's Telarigattu Ghat, the grey, hoary walls of Anegondi loom across the waters like a ghost from the past. Anegondi is the oldest surviving building of Hampi–Vijayanagar. Robert Sewell calls it 'the mother of the empire city'.

Fortunately for the nascent kingdom of Kampili, Kafur led one desultory campaign against it with rather indecisive results and before he could come back, events in Delhi completely changed the political scenario. His master Allauddin died. Kafur made a vain attempt to grab power by placing a puppet on the throne and was killed. The political anarchy in Delhi meant most of the Khalji forces stationed in the South were summoned to Delhi, giving the southern kingdoms a much needed breather.

The new dynasty that captured the Sultanate of Delhi was that of Ghiyasuddin Tughlak and he was keen to have Islam hold sway in the South. He sent his son Muhammad Jauna at the head of the Tughlak army but initially the campaign was not successful. Jauna's first siege of the Warangal fortress failed but the prince persisted and the Kakatiyas finally surrendered after a long fight. Then he marched southwards and annexed the Pandya kingdom which had been disturbed by internecine rivalry for years and placed a Muslim governor to rule Ma'bar from the city of Madura.

After his father was killed in a suspicious accident, Jauna came to the throne as Muhammad bin Tughlak and he would be remembered by posterity for his eccentric schemes, all of which failed. One of them was to shift his capital from Delhi to Devagiri, which he renamed as Daulatabad. For the southern kingdoms this was an ominous plan as it brought the Sultanate much closer. The Sultan had made a pragmatic decision as it would be easier to control the South from Daulatabad but he insisted that all the citizens of Delhi shift with him. The resistance of the people and the nobility ultimately made him move back to Delhi within a few years.

The temples on Hemakuta Hill are among the earliest shrines built in the Vijayanagar Empire.

Meanwhile in Kampili, King Kampiladeva began to assert himself. He resisted Tughlak demands for tribute and then as a final act of defiance he befriended a rebellious cousin of the Sultan and gave him refuge. Two attempts by Tughlak forces to defeat Kampiladeva failed but at the third attempt he was put under siege in the fortress of Anegondi. After a month, when food ran out he chose to die fighting and while he and his men surged out of the fort in a final assault, the royal women committed suicide in a fire. The kingdom of Kampili may not have lasted long but it laid the foundation of the Vijayanagar Empire that replaced it soon after.

Among the prisoners of war taken at Anegondi were two sons of a local chieftain named Sangama, who were treasury officers of Kampiladeva. When Harihara and his younger brother Bukka were marched away to Delhi their future seemed hopeless and few would have expected them to ever return. And no one would have imagined the great future that lay before the two men.

By the 1320s all the southern kingdoms, gravely weakened by decades of war, had become vassals of Delhi. However, the Sultanate rule had not taken roots in the region as the people had not accepted it. Smaller chieftains were always rising in rebellion across the South making the Tughlak presence a highly precarious one. One of the governors who constantly faced local uprisings was Malik Mohammad, the governor of Kampili and the troubled man soon lost the fort of Anegondi. Finally he wrote to the Sultan requesting that a new governor be sent to replace him and also suggested it should be someone who was familiar with the local situation.

Carvings of graceful dancers on the Mahanavami platform.

In the court of Delhi, Muhammad bin Tughlak had exactly the right men, two courtiers from Kampili—Harihara and his brother Bukka. The brothers had been forced to convert to Islam and were working at the royal court where they had won the Sultan's trust. They were now made to swear their allegiance to the Sultanate and sent back to Kampili as the new governors. Today the obscure little town of Kampili still survives 19 kilometres east of Hampi and there is nothing left to remind the visitor of its tumultuous history.

Two Brothers and a Saint...

For forty years, the sultans of Delhi had tried to subjugate the South and had failed to sustain their military successes. The southern kings would surrender or withdraw but once the Delhi armies went back, they rose again. Even at a time when wars were a part of life the people suffered terribly – villages and towns were sacked, thousands killed or taken away in slavery, temples were pillaged and then razed to the ground. This also coincided with the rise of a militant form of Shaivism that was inspired and led by many of the sages of the monastic orders – the various *math*s attached to shrines.

One of the most influential *math* was the Sringeri Sharada Peetha quite close to Kampili (*See* Box). This *math* was one of the four monastic orders established by the great scholar and sage Adi Shankaracharya in the 9th century AD. In the 1330s it was headed by a visionary scholar named Madhavacharya who later became the Shankaracharya and took the title of Vidyaranya. He played a crucial role in the lives of Harihara and Bukka who headed to Kampili as converts and agents of the Sultan of Delhi.

The early years of the brothers at Kampili and their association with Vidyaranya is now a mix of myths and legends that have come down through centuries. When they arrived at Kampili, they initially acted as the trusted lieutenants of the Sultan and did their best to pacify the people and establish peace in the region. However this phase did not last long and after meeting Vidyaranya they renounced Islam, returned to their old faith and then concentrated on establishing a Hindu kingdom. Among the declared aims of this new kingdom was the protection of Hindu dharma.

This kingdom came to be called Vijayanagar after its capital city though some inscriptions refer to the kingdom as 'Karnatak'. Vidyaranya was the mentor and adviser to the early kings and in many inscriptions the kings of Vijayanagar acknowledge his contributions to the empire. In one later inscription, in his memory, he is described as 'the supreme light incarnate'. This partnership of royalty and religion was a natural result of the anger felt by religious orders at the violent presence of Islam in the South. The anger was not just at the plundering of temples but also the danger they sensed towards the culture and traditions of the region as they had already seen how the ancient way of life had been battered in the North.

Ruins of buildings that once lined the banks of the Tungabhadra River.

So Vidyaranya not only advised the Sangama brothers, but also placed the substantial wealth and influence of the Sringeri Math at their disposal. A visionary and a shrewd observer of the political situation, he sensed that the old dynasties had depleted their strength fighting not just the Muslim foes but also each other. The only way the Islamic wave could be halted was by consolidating the various kingdoms into one powerful new empire. It was time to invest in younger talents and the far-sighted sage put his trust in the energy and enterprise of Sangama's two most talented sons.

Just as Vidyaranya needed Harihara and Bukka, the sage's support and blessings were absolutely essential to the brothers. As converts their social position was fragile and it would have been difficult for them to assert their power and gain acceptance as rulers as long as they remained Muslims. The sage now opened the way for them to return to the Hindu fold and his personal intervention was also essential to stop the opposition of other chieftains. When the revered head of the Sringeri Math personally converted Harihara and Bukka, few could protest.

The brothers celebrated their return to their ancestral faith by declaring their independence from Delhi and on an auspicious *Vijayadashami*, the tenth day of the Dussara festival in AD 1336, they laid the foundation of the capital of their Hindu kingdom at a site south of the Tungabhadra across the river from Anegondi. Vidyaranya as *kulaguru*, the family priest, crowned Harihara as the first king with his four brothers standing loyally by his side.

Circumstances also favoured the young kingdom. This was the time when the Hoysala king Ballala III, the most powerful ruler in the South, was killed fighting the Muslim kings of Madura, thus creating a vacuum that Vijayanagar quickly filled by gradually

annexing his kingdom. As one inscription says about Harihara I, 'the circle of earth belonging to the Hoysala family' had become 'an ornament on his arm'. As Robert Sewell writes in his seminal book *A Forgotten Empire*, 'The decayed old states crumbled away into nothingness and the fighting kings of Vijayanagar became the saviours of the South for two and a half centuries.'

At the same time, in the North, Muhammad bin Tughlak's reign drew to a close in a haze of confusion and the power of the Sultanate began to wane. He was succeeded by his cousin Ferozshah who was not interested in extending the kingdom. The Sultanate was deeply damaged by the invasion of Timur in AD 1398. The North plunged into a period of anarchy and the later sultans were weak. This political weakness gave the time to Vijayanagar to flourish in peace and at its zenith the Vijayanagar Empire spanned the whole of India south of the Krishna River. Its other boundaries were the Bay of Bengal in the east, the Arabian Sea in the west and the Indian Ocean in the south. As many of their inscriptions claimed, it truly spanned from sea to sea.

A parade of bejewelled dancers carved on a wall.

An aerial view of Hemakuta shrines with stone colonnades.

Harihara I became the first ruler of Vijayanagar and their line has come to be called the Sangama Dynasty. Bukka would play the role of his right-hand man and commander-in-chief. The other three brothers Kampana, Marappa and Mudappa acted as ministers and provincial governors. Vidyaranya became not just the spiritual preceptor, the *kulaguru,* of the Vijayanagar royal family but also at times acted as a minister.

In the early years, the sage had provided aid to the brothers and now the debt was paid back through generous grants of land to the Sringeri Math by the king. As historian S Shrikantaya writes, 'Sringeri became a state within a state, and its Guru a Rajaguru with a royal position. Titles and honours and the regalia of the State multiplied. *Agraharas* and temples and endowments and worships created a profound impression.' He also states, 'Instead of remaining a calm centre of learning, study, contemplation and penance, it became a State with officers to collect revenue and manage its affairs. The importance of this stronghold of the Advaita philosophy thus increased day after day.'

All the kings who followed took their role as protectors of the Hindu faith and culture as a divine responsibility. All across the South, temples that had been destroyed were repaired and their worship revived again and many new ones were built. They actively patronised cultural traditions in literature, architecture, sculpture, music and dance and thus the city of Vijayanagar became the cultural heart of the South. The rise of Vijayanagar came just in time – within the next fifteen years, a new Islamic power would rise in north Deccan, that of the Bahmani Dynasty.

Following page: *Painted ceiling of the gorgeous coronation* mandapa *in the Virupaksha Temple.*

They named their new city Vijayanagar (City of Victory) and also Vidyanagar (City of Learning) in grateful commemoration of their guru and it was completed by AD 1343. The selection of the site, south of the Tungabhadra was also a practical one as the terrain offered protection against invasions. The wide, torrential river was impassable at most points and created a perfect northern boundary and the city was encircled by low, craggy hills and a landscape strewn with giant boulders that acted like a natural fortress. This forbidding terrain of the Tungabhadra River flowing through hills would save Vijayanagar many times in the future.

The myth about the selection of this specific site tells the story of Harihara going out with his hounds to hunt for rabbit near the Tungabhadra. As his dogs chased their prey, Harihara saw an amazing sight – one of the fleeing rabbits suddenly turned around and bit one of the hounds. He reported what he had seen to Vidyaranya who interpreted it as an auspicious sign and advised him to lay the foundation of his new city at the spot where a gentle rabbit had stood up to a fierce hound. The symbolism in the tale is clear enough – the old civilisation and religion would stand its ground here and fight the incursions from the North.

The reigning deities of the city were Lord Virupaksha, who is a form of Lord Shiva and his consort Goddess Pampa, an aspect of Parvati. They are still worshipped at the Virupaksha Temple, whose *gopuram* soars at one end of the Hampi Bazaar. It is the oldest shrine at Hampi and probably it was already there when the city was built. Its stone *mandapa*s and *garbha griha* still echo to the ringing of bells and the chanting of mantras in an eternal ritual of worship. In a typical act of tolerance and syncretism, Virupakasha, a form of Lord Shiva, became the royal family's deity while the royal crest was of the Varaha, an avatar of Lord Vishnu, the God of Preservation. You can see the chunky figure of the boar crest carved all across the city.

At the same time this revival of a Hindu kingdom was carried out in a splendid spirit of tolerance as people of all faiths were welcomed and allowed to live peacefully within the kingdom. In the medieval world, an alliance between the king and the religious establishment to build an empire has happened often but this is one of the rare instances where it came coloured with an amazing attitude of acceptance of all other faiths. There is not a single instance when a mosque or church was destroyed by a Vijayanagar king. What they created was a vibrant, cosmopolitan empire where Arab traders and Portuguese sailors wandered in its markets, Jains built their own temples and the king had Muslim soldiers in his army who were allowed to take their oath of allegiance over the Koran.

The coronation of Harihara must have been an occasion with great promise. In Nilakanta Sastri's vivid words,

> *Here, in the presence of God Virupaksha, Harihara I celebrated his coronation in the proper Hindu style on 18th April 1336. He undertook the rule of the kingdom as the agent of the deity to whom all the land south of the Krishna River was supposed to belong, and his successors kept up the practice he started by authenticating all their acts of state by the sign manual of Sri Virupaksha.*

In their inscriptions, Harihara and Bukka called themselves by the comparatively modest title of *Mahamandalesvara* (the King of a Region); it is the later rulers who would dub themselves with high flown titles of *Maharajadhiraja* (King of kings) and *Rajaparamesvara* (King and God).

Within a decade, the energetic sons of Sangama had conquered many areas including most of the old Hoysala kingdom.

In AD 1346, the entire family of the five brothers and their chief relatives and lieutenants could meet at Sringeri, the seat of the Hindu pontiff, to celebrate the conquest of dominions extending from sea to sea by holding a great festival (*vijayotsava*) in the presence of the most eminent spiritual leaders of the Hindu community.

The magnificent and variegated history of Vijayanagar had begun.

Facing page top: *Ceiling painting showing Lord Ram in his chariot going out to battle with demon-king Ravana.*

Facing page bottom: *A painted panel on the ceiling of the Virupaksha Temple, showing an episode from the Ramayana.*

A wall of rocks that was part of the defences of Vijayanagar, as it circled and protected the city for centuries.

VIDYARANYA OF SRINGERI

The Vedic scholar and sage Adi Shankaracharya led a great revival of Hinduism in the 9th century AD. He began his missionary journey from the village of Kaladi in Kerala, where he was born and visited most of the important sacred centres of the land. He would die at the other end of the subcontinent, in Badrinath, high in the Himalayan ranges of Uttarakhand. His philosophy of Advaita Vedanta transformed and revitalised the ancient Brahmanical religion.

He established four centres of learning and pontifical seats at the four cardinal points of the land. At Joshimath in Uttarakhand, Dwarka in Gujarat, Puri in Orissa and the Sharada Peetha at Sringeri in Karnataka. Later a fifth, the Kamakoti Peetha would function at Kanchipuram in Tamil Nadu. It is Sringeri that would play a vital role in the foundation of Vijayanagar.

The Sharada Peetha was established at a picturesque spot by the banks of the Tungabhadra in the Chikmagulur District of modern Karnataka. It is the oldest of all the *math*s. Adi Shankaracharya's mission of preserving and propagating Hinduism is still carried out here. The followers of Advaita Vedanta follow the Vedic phrase *aham Brahma asmi*, ('I am the universal spirit'). According to their philosophy of non dualism, Shiva is Vishnu and Vishnu is Shiva. Both are one and the same. It was this spirit of synergetic tolerance that suffused the rulers of Vijayanagar.

The main temple at Sringeri is of the Goddess Sharada, a form of Saraswati, the Goddess of Learning and Music, who inspired the Vedas. The gurus at the *math* are all Vedic scholars who are dedicated to the revival and preservation of our ancient philosophy and literature. The present Shankaracharya is the 36th in an unbroken line of *acharya*s.

At the time of the invasions of Malik Kafur, the Sringeri Math was headed by Vidyateertha Muni. He had three talented *shishya*s—the brothers Madhava, Sayana and Bhoganatha. Vidyateertha sent them on missions across the South to speak to the people and visit the rulers of the region in an effort to persuade them to unite into a Hindu confederacy to fight the threat from the North. When Harihara and Bukka arrived in Kampili as the envoys of the Tughlaks, Madhavacharya met them and saw in them the potential to establish such an empire.

First he convinced the brothers to renounce their allegiance to the Tughlaks and return to the Hindu fold and he personally converted them back to Hinduism. The wealth and influence of the Sringeri Math was now harnessed to the purpose of laying the foundation of their kingdom and its new capital city. Later, this generosity would be returned many fold with generous grants of land to the Sharada Peetha by many kings of Vijayanagar. By the time the city rose around AD 1336, Madhavacharya had become the Shankaracharya and taken the title of Vidyaranya, 'Forest of Learning'. He was the twenty-second *acharya* of the *math*. His brother Sayana became a formidable scholar of the Vedas and his commentaries are referred to even today.

The myths about the foundation of the city show the vital role played by Madhavacharya-Vidyaranya. It is he who selected the location where the rabbit rebelled and bit the hound that was chasing it. Also there is the myth that Vidyaranya prayed to Goddess Bhuvaneshwari asking for the wealth that would be needed to establish a new city. The goddess was so pleased with his prayers that she showered him with gold. Vidayranya was the *kulaguru*, the spiritual preceptor and adviser to both Harihara and Bukka. The latter took an active interest in the revival of Vedic studies and with Vidyaranya he was the patron of Sayana, who worked with a team of *pandit*s to produce his monumental work, *Sarvadarsana-sangraha*, a brilliant study of Advaita philosophy.

With the encouragement of Vidyaranya, temples like the shrine at Srirangam that had been destroyed by the armies of the Sultanate were repaired and new ones were built. The tradition was continued by later kings and Tirupati, Srirangam, Chidambaram, Rameshwaram, Madurai – every major shrine received their patronage. Vidyaranya died in AD 1386 and by then the Vijayanagar kingdom was flourishing. In the early years, the city was also known as Vidyanagar in acknowledgement of its patron saint.

Vijayanagar is the 'City of Victory', Vidyanagar is the 'City of Learning'—the two names capture the spirit of the kingdom that Vidyaranya inspired.

Chapter Three

FROM ZENITH TO OBLIVION

History of the greatest years of the Vijayanagar Empire

That great empire which by resisting the onslaught of Islam championed the cause of Hindu civilisation and culture in the South for close upon three centuries and thus preserved the ancient traditions of the country in its polity, its learning and its arts. The history of Vijayanagar is the last glorious chapter in the history of independent Hindu South India.

– Nilakanta Sastri

3

The first two decades of the history of Vijayanagar was a time for laying the foundation of a kingdom that would one day spread across the Deccan Peninsula and become an empire. The laying of the roots of that empire was the most important achievement of its first two kings—Harihara I and then his younger brother Bukka I. The challenge was not just the conquest and consolidation of the land but also establishing the basis of good administration and peace in which both trade and agriculture could flourish. So the consequent wealth of the kingdom and the prosperity of the people would be based on the pragmatic foresight of the sons of Sangama.

Power and ambition are always divisive factors within a royal family but it was not so with the first two Vijayanagar kings. Few historians take note of one remarkable fact—the unity and cooperation that continued between the five brothers even after Harihara had taken the throne and then the smooth transition to the reign of Bukka. This is in great contrast to the later years when the empire was weakened by the internecine conflict within the royal family and was one of the causes of its eventual eclipse. Each

The double-storied gateway of the Telarigattu Ghat; it was once the main landing for boats and ships coming to Vijayanagar.

Facing page: *Horses and war elephants were greatly valued by the warrior kings of Vijayanagar. Here the majestic Elephant Stables that stand in the Royal Enclosure.*

brother was given an important province to govern and functioned quite independently. Bukka was designated as the *uparaja* or co-regent, and as one inscription mentions, he was the 'prop of the throne' and had his seat in the powerful principality of Gutti.

The Sangama Dynasty...

Harihara was wise enough to nominate Bukka as his successor and so, at his death in AD 1356, there was a smooth and peaceful transition of power. Bukka I would rule for the next two decades and historians call their dynasty the Sangama Dynasty after their father, about whom we really know very little. The reign of the Sangamas lasted nearly a century and a half, from AD 1336 to AD 1485 and included a galaxy of powerful kings like Deva Raya I and II. Interestingly, the growing influence and confidence of this fledgling kingdom is reflected in a small entry in the royal records of the Ming Dynasty in distant China. In AD 1374, Bukka Raya I sent a royal embassy to the court of the Ming emperor which was 'received with honour'.

Painted stone carving of Hanuman at Telarigattu Ghat.

The history of Vijayanagar, right from its beginnings, is one of conflict with its neighbours. In the early years, its greatest adversary was the Bahmani kingdom in the north with its capital at Gulbarga. The

Facing page: *The* gopuram *of the Virupaksha Temple. The Vijayanagar kings claimed to rule in the name of Lord Virupaksha.*

Pages 70–71: *The basements of palaces and remnants of the surrounding fortifications in the Royal Enclosure.*

Bahmanis and the Sangamas would battle constantly for the fertile river valleys between the Krishna and the Tungabhadra rivers called the Raichur Doab. Also there were powerful local chieftains like the Reddis of Rajahmundry, the Velamas of Telengana, the Sultan of Madura and a few years later, the rising ambitions of the Gajapati kings of Orissa. They were always on the lookout for opportunities to invade. The Vijayanagar kings became masters at playing off these various centres of power, allying with one and then another and maintained a huge standing army that was always ready to head out to war. At its zenith, during the reign of the warrior-king Krishnadeva Raya, Vijayanagar succeeded in vanquishing all of them.

Chakratirtha, the most sacred bathing place on the River Tungabhadra.

The Bahmani kingdom in north Deccan was the most dangerous of them all and it had risen out of the disintegration of the Sultanate at Delhi and the withdrawal of northern forces. The battle between the Bahmani and Vijayanagar rulers was the most serious one – it was for gaining sovereignty over the whole Peninsula, especially its fertile lands and ports along the west coast that was a source of lucrative trade.

Bukka I would face the attacks of Bahmani sultans Muhammad I and Mujahid and Vijayanagar did not fare too well in the conflict. The hero of his reign was his son Kumara Kampana who was a successful general. Kampana's greatest military triumph was the defeat of the sultans of Madura in AD 1370 and the annexation of the region where he then ruled as the governor. His military campaigns are enshrined in an exquisite Sanskrit epic poem called *Madhura Vijayam* (The Conquest of Madura) that was composed by Kampana's wife Ganga Devi. Fortunately the poem has survived and in it Ganga Devi writes that Kampana had a dream in which Meenakshi, the Goddess of Madura, begged him to rescue the land and sent him a sacred sword.

Once Kampana had established the rule of Vijayanagar in the Madura region, he restored all the temples that had been destroyed by the sultans. The image of Lord Raghunatha that had been carried away for safe keeping was once again placed in the sanctum of the Srirangam shrine. This was welcomed by the people with great fanfare and this established a tradition among the later Vijayanagar kings of energetically patronising the building and restoration of temples. Even today one can see inscriptions recording their generosity on the walls and gateways of temples all across South India. Tragically Kampana died in AD 1374. By the end of the reign of Bukka I, a large area had come under the Vijayanagar kingdom including Nellore, Mangalore and the strategically important port of Goa.

All the important temples had a bazaar attached to them. Here the ruins of an arcade of shops near the Vitthala Temple.

As N Venkataramanayya writes about Bukka I, he was 'the real architect of the Vijayanagar Empire. He was a great soldier and achieved conspicuous success on the field of battle ... in an age marked by religious bigotry and fanaticism, special reference must be made to the policy of tolerance adopted by Bukka I.' He took an active interest in the revival of the Vedic dharma and assumed the title of *Vedamarga pratishthapaka* – the establisher of the path of the Vedas – and gathered scholars under his guru Vidyaranya and his brother Sayanacharya who composed new commentaries on the Vedas.

Bukka I was succeeded by his son Harihara II and his reign of twenty-seven years was a time of both consolidation and conflict. The ports on the Arabian Sea like Goa, Chaul and Dabhol that were crucial for trade with the West were annexed, bringing with it a rise in both revenue and trade. Harihara II's son Virupaksha even led a successful expedition to the island of Sri Lanka. However, the northern frontier remained unsettled with frequent skirmishes with the Bahmani sultans. In AD 1398, Firuz Bahmani pursued the Vijayanagar army into the city leading to a terrible massacre. He only withdrew after extracting a ruinous ransom for the prisoners of war and forcing a humiliating treaty on Vijayanagar.

A watchtower that shows architectural influences of the Islamic style.

After a short period of chaos when two princes Virupaksha and Bukka captured and then lost the throne, Deva Raya I ascended the Diamond Throne of Vijayanagar and ruled for sixteen eventful years. It was during his reign that the Italian traveller Nicolo dei Conti arrived at Vijayanagar and left a fascinating account of the city, its people and their rather colourful monarch. Deva Raya was the first great builder of the dynasty and extended the boundaries of the city by building another line of walls pierced by towered gateways. He also started the exquisite Vitthala Temple that would be added to by many other kings. Deva Raya's greatest building work was a dam across the Tungabhadra that boosted agriculture in the region. Robert Sewell, writing in 1890, says that it was a

> *great work … construction of a huge dam in the Tungabhadra River, and the formation of an aqueduct fifteen miles long from the river to the city. If this be the same channel that to the present day supplies the fields which occupy so much of the site of the old city, it is a most extraordinary work. For several miles this channel is cut out of the solid rock at the base of the hills, and is one of the most remarkable irrigation works to be seen in India.*

Even today one can see sections of the dam and parts of the aqueduct snaking across the ruins at Hampi.

Sultan Firuz Bahmani continued his hostilities towards Vijayanagar in Deva Raya's reign and this led to years of conflict that brought an equal share of victories and defeats to Vijayanagar and the Bahmanis. However, it ultimately ended in Deva Raya's

Ruins of the encircling fortifications of Vijayanagar and a tower that still keeps watch over the desolate landscape.

humiliation when he had to give up a strategic fortress and also agree to give his daughter in marriage to Firuz. There is a popular story recounted by the historian Ferishta about how Deva Raya's passion for a farmer's daughter led to the war (*See* Box). It did not help Deva Raya that some of the Reddi chieftains chose to ally with Firuz and Deva Raya lost the Raichur Doab region. Historians point out that Ferishta is the only historian who mentions the treaty that forced Deva Raya to send his daughter to Firuz's harem; none of the contemporary Hindu or Muslim historians do so. Ferishta wrote much later in the early years of the 17th century while staying at Bijapur and depended entirely on documentary and oral sources. True or just bazaar gossip, his tale of a marriage procession of a sultan into Vijayanagar makes for interesting reading!

The early years of Deva Raya's rule were spent in conflict with not just the Bahmani and Reddi chieftains but also the rising power

The stone basement of a palace in the Royal Enclosure; the superstructure made of bricks and wood has vanished.

of the Gajapati kings of Orissa. The battles were always centred at the hilltop fortresses that dominated a region. For example, the Bahmani forces laid siege to the fortress of Pangal for two years till Deva Raya arrived with a large army and as the fort's garrison swept out of the hill bastion, Deva Raya attacked from behind. As they sandwiched the Sultan's army between them, they forced Firuz to flee and for a while established Vijayanagar's sovereignty over the Krishna–Tungabhadra Doab.

The delicately moulded alcoves overhanging the empty pool of the Queen's Bath.

Deva Raya's reign is one of the most magnificent of the Sangama Dynasty. For fifty years, first as the prince and then as king, he strengthened the administration and the army of his kingdom that had by now become big enough to be called an empire. He was the first to study the military success of the Muslim armies and realise that their greatest advantage lay in their swiftly moving cavalry. He began the Vijayanagar tradition of investing in good horses and then in the latest artillery. Arab traders brought the finest Arab and Persian horses to the port of Goa and then sold them to Vijayanagar. Later the trade would be monopolised by the Portuguese and this led to the presence of Portuguese traders in the city. This became a historical serendipity that would lead to the memoirs of trader-travellers like Domingo Paes and Fernao Nuniz that today give us such a detailed portrait of the city and its people.

Deva Raya like most of the Vijayanagar rulers was a pragmatic and tolerant man and recruitment in his army was based on ability. He employed Turkish archers and Muslim soldiers who were offered land and money and permitted to live freely within the kingdom. They took their oath of allegiance on the Holy Koran and mosques were built by them in localities that must have been quite large as Domingo Paes called them 'the Moorish quarters'. This easy-going tolerance was in sharp contrast to the regions ruled by the sultans where temples were frequently raided for their wealth and often destroyed. This policy of modernising

the army and maintaining well-trained standing forces ultimately helped Deva Raya I to emerge victorious from the constant skirmishes with Firuz Shah and also keep the Gajapati under control.

Deva Raya reigned for sixteen years and the last years were peaceful, allowing him to indulge in his creative and cultural interests. He cherished scholarship and surrounded himself with poets, philosophers and musicians and the artists who pleased him were invited to the Pearl Hall of the palace and showered with gold coins and precious gems. The shower of coins has entered the legends of the South and references can be found centuries later in Telugu and Kannada literature. Thus Vijayanagar became a true Vidyanagar, a centre of learning and culture, where the finest creative talents gathered. Deva Raya was a devotee of Lord Shiva and his consort the Goddess Pampa and also built temples dedicated to the deities.

There is often a period of chaos when a strong king leaves the scene and that is what happened when Deva Raya died in AD 1422. There was a struggle for the throne between two of his sons Ramachandra and Vijaya I. During Vijaya's short reign the real centre of power was his son the prince-regent Deva Raya who took the Diamond Throne

Carvings of a triumphant Lord Hanuman leaping over the sea to the kingdom of Lanka can be seen everywhere.

Facing page: *Among the many mythical creatures carved on the walls of temples, the half-lion, half-horse* yali *is the most eye-catching.*

of Vijayanagar as Deva Raya II in AD 1424. Just like his grandfather and namesake's rule, his reign was a period of constant conflict with the neighbouring kingdoms, with absolute victory eluding both sides. However, this did not prevent the empire from flourishing. When he died in AD 1446, Deva Raya II's empire extended from the Krishna River in the north to Sri Lanka in the south and from sea to sea – the Arabian Sea in the west to the Bay of Bengal in the east.

Tribute and revenue poured into the coffers of the monarch not just from the land but from busy ports along both coasts and now Vijayanagar also had an active navy to protect its trade. Caesaro Federici, the Italian traveller describes the trade and writes,

> *The Merchandize that went every yeere from Goa to Bezeneger were Arabian Horses, Velvets, Damaskes and Sattens, Armesine of Porugall and pieces of China, Saffron and Scarlets; and from Bezeneger they had in Turkie for their commodities, Jwels and Pagodies which be Ducats of Gold.*

As Vijayanagar flourished, Deva Raya II, just like his grandfather, also patronised the arts and held glittering literary and philosophical soirees, built temples and added new palaces to the royal quarters of the city.

The Persian traveller Abdur Razzaq visited Vijayanagar during the reign of Deva Raya II and has written about the attempt made on the life of Deva Raya in AD 1446 by a cousin. The king and his noblemen were invited to a feast and then attacked with knives. May be sensing danger, Deva Raya had cancelled his visit at the last minute but the perfidious cousin managed to enter his palace and stabbed the

Even the plinths of the temples are adorned with intricate carvings.

Raya with a poisoned knife. The king fought back, called for help and the assassin was killed. However Deva Raya was seriously wounded and died a few months later.

After Deva Raya II, the Sangama Dynasty drifted into a series of weak kings, there was much intrigue within the royal family with a number of princes simultaneously claiming the throne and at times even holding court at the same period. One king was assassinated by his cousin who usurped the throne and then soon lost it. A volatile situation at the centre meant that all their enemies raised their heads. The Gajapati claimed the coastal Andhra region and quickly occupied the strategically crucial forts of Udayagiri, Chandragiri and Tiruchirapalli, deeply damaging the prestige of the Rayas of Vijayanagar. The powerful local chieftains began to assert their independence. The Bahmanis captured Goa affecting both trade and the supply of horses to Vijayanagar. The saviour of the kingdom was a nobleman named Saluva Narasimha who finally moved to control the reins of power and end the anarchy before Vijayanagar was destroyed.

The Saluva Dynasty...

Saluva Narasimha was the powerful governor of Chittoor and as a regent he officially acted for the king, maintaining one feeble Raya after another on the throne, but he was in fact the real centre of power. He first began a campaign against Orissa, recaptured Udayagiri and controlled the uprisings of rebellious chieftains. Then after winning over the nobility, he finally ascended to the throne in AD 1485, with the last Sangama king, Praudha Deva Raya fleeing before his advancing forces.

Saluva Narasimha's reign of six tumultuous years was spent in trying to hold the empire together and all through his rule he was constantly on the march against rebellious noblemen. When he died in AD 1490 his two sons were very young and the commander-in-chief Narasa Nayaka acted as their guardian and regent and at least for appearances sake kept one prince on the throne. He continued with the job of re-establishing Vijayanagar's rule in Andhra and Tamil regions. In one matter Narasa Nayaka was unique in the annals of Vijayanagar royalty—he

would be the father of three kings who followed—Vira Narasimha, Krishnadeva and Achyuta. Even Sangama had fathered two! When Narasa Nayaka died, the throne was captured by his son Vira Narasimha who started the Tuluva Dynasty which would produce the finest among all Vijayanagar monarchs – the warrior-king Krishnadeva Raya.

Pages 86, 87: *Sculptures that are now preserved in the Hampi Museum.*

Pavilions line the Bazaar pathway and lead to the granite steps of Matanga Hill.

The Tuluva Dynasty...

All through his reign Narasa Nayaka had maintained the fiction that the sons of Saluva Narasimha were the kings of Vijayanagar, when in fact the two boys spent their lives in virtual captivity. However his son Vira Narasimha had no such scruples and in AD 1505 the last Saluva king was assassinated in the Penugonda Fort where the poor young man had spent most of his life. Thus the dynasty called Tuluva now officially occupied the Diamond Throne of Vijayanagar.

The five-year reign of Vira Narasimha was a period of turmoil as both the nobility and his subjects were unhappy with the ruthless manner in which he had usurped the throne. Some of the noblemen even chose to ally with the Bahmani sultan Mahmud Shah who was planning another jihad against the heathens of Vijayanagar and in this he was being egged on by a rising new power, the ruler of Bijapur, Yusuf Adil Khan. Initially, the Sultan's army faced little opposition and captured Raichur and Mudgal but then Vira Narasimha marched out and inflicted a crushing defeat on them. Vira Narasimha may not have been a popular king but he was an energetic and pragmatic one. He was having problems getting horses from Arab traders as they preferred to sell to Bijapur and so he allied with the Portuguese, sending an envoy to Governor Almeida. This support played a crucial role in the Portuguese grabbing the lucrative horse trade and would tie up the prosperity of Goa with the survival of Vijayanagar.

Vira Narasimha died in AD 1509 and was succeeded by his half-brother Krishnadeva. The Portuguese chroniclers say that Vira Narasimha did not want Krishnadeva to succeed him even though his own sons were much too young to become king. While on his

The courtyard of the Vitthala Temple with a view of the maha mandapa *(right) and the* kalyana mandapa *(left).*

deathbed, he ordered his minister Saluva Timma to assassinate Krishnadeva but Saluva did not do so, thus ensuring a smooth transition at the king's death. Saluva Timma became Krishnadeva Raya's closest adviser, chief minister and also a leading general. In a history that echoes a mythical tragedy, Saluva Timma played an important role in the success of his protégé and also became a source of great sorrow in the last years of Krishnadeva Raya's reign.

The Warrior-King Krishnadeva Raya...

The new Raya faced a phalanx of enemies in the north and the remnants of rebellions within the kingdom. The Bahmani kingdom was slowly disintegrating under a series of ineffectual kings and soon powerful provincial governors began to break away to establish their own kingdoms. The five kingdoms that would finally emerge from the ruins of the Bahmani kingdom were of Bijapur, Ahmednagar, Golconda, Bidar and Berar and among them Bijapur, that shared a frontier with Vijayanagar, was the most aggressively inimical to the Rayas. So while Krishnadeva Raya faced the persistent animosity of Yusuf Adil Khan on one side, the Gajapati, Prataparudra of Orissa was constantly on the look out to capture the eastern districts of Vijayanagar.

As always, a new untested king and a time of uncertainty in Vijayanagar was the perfect time to announce another jihad. So in AD 1509, within a few months of Krishnadeva's coronation, at the instigation of Yusuf Adil Khan, the Bahmani sultan Mahmud once again headed south at the head of a vast army. Their calculations went terribly wrong as they faced a crushing defeat with Mahmud himself being wounded and having to flee from the battlefield. As the Sultan's forces began to retreat Krishnadeva chased them and defeated them again in another encounter. Then at the Battle of Kovelakonda, Yusuf Adil Khan was killed and the infant state of Bijapur was thrown into disorder, giving Vijayanagar a few years of peace.

Krishnadeva was not through yet and Vijayanagar marched on, recovering many lost regions like the Raichur Doab and even advanced into Gulbarga, the capital of the Bahmanis and then moved towards Bidar and captured its fort. After putting his stamp on the opposition's land he then chose to withdraw but only after restoring Mahmud Shah on the Bahmani throne. This was a shrewd move because the governors who were trying to break away from the Bahmani kingdom now had to contend with the survival of the Bahmani Dynasty. Returning to Vijayanagar, Krishnadeva Raya assumed a new title that said it all – *Yavana-rajya-sthapan-acharya* – the lord who establishes a king in the kingdom of the heathens.

View of the ruins of a gopuram *and old bazaar colonnades as seen from the Vitthala Temple.*

Four years later, in AD 1513, Krishnadeva felt strong enough to move against Prataparudra of Orissa. The Gajapati was holding on to two important eastern provinces – Udayagiri and Kondavidu that earlier Vijayanagar kings had failed to recover. Capturing the Udayagiri Fort was going to be a very tough enterprise as it was a formidable citadel built on a steep hill and hearing of the advancing Vijayanagar forces, the Gajapati sent a vast army to stop them but Krishnadeva was prepared. First the Oriya forces were defeated and pursued out of the province and then he turned to face the challenge of seizing Udayagiri.

The siege of Udayagiri showed the military genius of Krishnadeva who always moved according to a definite military plan and like all

Aerial view of the Danaik Enclosure.

great generals he was a shrewd and patient man. He studied the terrain and immediately spotted the main problem. There was only one road up the hill to the entrance of the fort, a narrow, steep hill path that was just broad enough for one man to pass, thus making advancing soldiers easy targets for the archers waiting behind the high battlements. At the first sign of an advancing army there would be a barrage of rocks and arrows from above. So first the road was widened and then all exit points from where the Oriya garrison could escape was blocked with high stone ramparts. Seeing the phalanx of Vijayanagar soldiers marching up and their escape route blocked, the fort garrison promptly surrendered.

On his way back from Udayagiri, Krishnadeva and his two chief queens Chinna Devi and Tirumale Devi visited the Venkateshwara Temple at Tirupati. He gifted much gold and jewels to the temple and the standing images of the king and his two queens still stand in an outer hall of the temple. He also brought back the image of Balagopal from Udayagiri and built the Krishna Temple in Vijayanagar where the idol was placed.

Krishnadeva was not done yet. He returned in triumph to Vijayanagar but soon marched out again to recapture the province of Kondavidu. One fort after another fell and the Oriya forces fled in panic. The garrison stationed within the Kondavidu Fort still held out and at first were successful in resisting an attack by Saluva Timma. Then Krishnadeva arrived and devised a new way to lay siege to the fort. High wooden platforms were built called *nada-chapparams* that were then carried right below the fort walls. Then as the men behind the ramparts watched in horror, the Vijayanagar soldiers climbed up to the platforms and fought the opposition face to face and swordsmen clambered across the walls. At the same time, parts of the walls were broken or seized by soldiers moving up the ladders and the fort was taken.

Many prisoners were taken at Kondavidu and among them was Prince Virabhadra, the son and heir of Prataparudra and one of his queens and many noblemen. They were all taken to Vijayanagar where the imprisoned prince later committed suicide. While Vijayanagar was laying siege to Kondavidu, the Vijayanagar army had also faced a new danger. The Gajapati had hurried out of Orissa in an attempt to attack from behind. Krishnadeva promptly turned his army around to face the new threat and even though they were attacked by the Gajapati while crossing a river, they routed the Oriya forces and watched them flee in disarray. Then with amazing calmness Krishnadeva turned around and went back to the siege and soon captured the Kondavidu Fort.

Pillared hall of the Pattabhirama Temple which was built by one of the queens of King Achyut Raya.

To stamp his sovereignty over the eastern provinces, Krishnadeva now marched through the region and at one point his army had to travel through a hilly area. Here the Gajapati's general Shitab Khan placed sixty thousand archers across the narrow mountain passes. Krishnadeva used his cavalry to climb up the hills surrounding the passes and surprised Shitab Khan with an attack from above and behind, forcing him to retreat. Rajahmundry... Vengi... Simhachalam... the triumphant Vijayanagar army marched on. In spite of such convincing defeats, Prataparudra was still unwilling to acknowledge the sovereignty of Vijayanagar. So Krishnadeva entered the Oriya capital Cuttack and then at the news of his son having committed suicide in captivity the Gajapati finally sued for peace. A treaty was concluded in AD 1518 according to which he gave one of his daughters in marriage to Krishnadeva (*See* Box). The Raya was magnanimous in victory and returned the land north of the Krishna River that he had earlier conquered to his vanquished enemy.

Even now the travails of Vijayanagar were not over. As the Gajapati's forces withdrew, the Golconda army of Quli Qutub Shah and Bijapur forces led by Ismail Adil Khan moved across the frontier in a two-pronged attack. Saluva Timma decisively defeated Golconda at the Battle of Kondavidu, captured the commander and his officers and sent them back to Vijayanagar as prisoners. Krishnadeva dealt a crushing defeat to Bijapur and the Sultan fled leaving all his cannons and army camp behind. Now Krishnadeva laid siege to the Raichur Fort and captured it. Here he was helped by the Portuguese musketeers led by Christovao de Figueiredo. These sharp shooters created havoc as they picked out the men moving along the fort walls. Later at the

Mahanavami festival in Vijayanagar, Figueiredo was honoured with gifts by the king. Domingo Paes who was a member of his entourage has left behind a fascinating description of the celebrations.

When an envoy of Bijapur arrived at Vijayanagar protesting against the Raya's invasion and demanding the return of Bijapur land, Krishnadeva's disdainful reply was that he would do so if Ismail Adil Khan would come and kiss his feet. The Sultan agreed to do so and then failed to appear at the place of meeting on the borders of the two kingdoms. A furious Raya then swept into the city of Bijapur and sacked the capital as Ismail Adil Khan fled.

Krishnadeva Raya had finally established himself as the unchallenged sovereign of southern India and did not face any more attacks from his obstreperous neighbours. Finally, peace was won and the last decade of his reign was a time when the city flourished. However, the last days of the king were darkened by personal tragedy. Krishnadeva had two principal queens—Tirumale Devi and Chinna Devi. For a long time he did not have an heir till Tirumale Devi gave birth to a son in AD 1518, named Tirumala Deva. While his son was still an infant, Krishnadeva decided to crown him king and and he himself ruled as his regent. However eight months after his coronation, the child-king died.

A sorrowful Krishnadeva Raya was told by noblemen that Tirumala Deva had been poisoned by Timma Dandanayaka and for Krishnadeva this was a great shock as he was the son of Saluva Timma who was his most trusted adviser. Krishnadeva was so close to him that he called Saluva 'appaji' or father. For reasons that are unclear Krishnadeva believed the report and Saluva and his two sons were imprisoned. Dandanayaka escaped and tried to raise a revolt but was captured. Then Saluva Timma and his sons were blinded and the old man died soon after. When he fell ill, a deeply saddened Krishnadeva Raya chose his brother Achyuta as his successor. After an illustrious reign of two decades, one of the greatest monarchs of medieval India died in AD 1529 and his brother who had spent years in captivity in a fortress during the reign of Krishnadeva emerged to sit on the Diamond Throne of Vijayanagar.

Entrance pavilion to the Vitthala Temple tank.

The Waning Years...

After the majestic, multifaceted qualities of Krishnadeva Raya, there was a sad decline in both character and ability of the later kings of Vijayanagar. Krishnadeva died in AD 1529 and by AD 1565 the great empire lay in ruins. His successor and half-brother Achyuta Raya faced the opposition and intrigue of the powerful noblemen Rama Raya who was married to Krishnadeva's daughter. From then on there were two centres of power in the empire—the ruling king and Rama Raya—and this weakened the authority of the royal family.

At one point Rama Raya even imprisoned Achyuta Raya and he replaced the old bureaucracy with men who were only loyal to him. One result of this was that the old bureaucrats now intrigued against the royal family leading to divisions among the nobility. Many of the generals loyal to Achyuta Raya were sacked and replaced by Muslim mercenaries and these men would one day betray Rama Raya at the crucial battle at Talikota. Watching the atmosphere of intrigue and disunity and sensing this weakness, the neighbouring kings moved in to capture strategic forts and areas. Bijapur claimed Raichur and Mudgal; the Gajapati and Golconda invaded; the Portuguese were rising in the west coast and now without the fear of Vijayanagar they attacked smaller Hindu kingdoms to pillage and destroy temples.

A series of kings followed but the power lay in the tenacious hands of Rama Raya, who also interfered in the internal affairs of the neighbouring sultanates creating greater antagonism. Meanwhile the five southern sultanates were cementing relationships through marriage alliances and finally it led to a joint campaign against Vijayanagar. The combined forces of Bijapur, Golconda, Ahmednagar, Bidar and Berar reached the fort of Talikota in AD 1565. Some historians call this the Battle of Rakshasi-Tangadi as it was fought between two villages called Rakkasige and Tangadige. In the decisive battle on 23 January 1565, two Muslim commanders of Vijayanagar deserted the battlefield and Rama Raya was defeated. He was captured and beheaded and after this the Vijayanagar soldiers

In the villages surrounding Hampi, people live among the ruins of Vijayanagar.

turned and fled. The road to the city now lay open before the invaders and the defenceless citizens had no option but to flee and they were led by the last official king of the Tuluva Dynasty, Sadashiva.

In the utter chaos that followed the enemy soldiers and local criminal tribes descended on the city to loot, massacre and destroy with vicious abandon. No one knows how many died but the mark of the destruction can still be seen on the walls of ruined temples – the beautiful images that were smashed with hammers, the dark smudges on the ceilings from fires, the gates and walls turned to rubble. After months of this dance of death what remained was the shell of a magnificent metropolis. As Sewell writes about the horrific fall of Vijayanagar, while looking at the ruins all around him,

> *With fire and sword, with crowbars and axes, they carried on day after day their work of destruction. Never perhaps in the history of the world has such havoc been wrought, and wrought suddenly, on so splendid a city, teeming with a wealthy and industrious population in the full plenitude of prosperity one day, and on the next seized, pillaged and reduced to ruins amid scenes of savage massacres and horrors beggaring description.*

As a Sangam poet Perunkunrar Kilar wrote about war,

> *Your armies move*
> *Murderous bull-elephants,*
> *Rows of shields*
> *Splendour of white flags waving on chariots.*
> *And the parade is a great pleasure*
> *to onlookers.*

But as it overruns and destroys enemy lands,
To bring back a booty of ornaments
It spells evil to the men in the camps
Of those kings
who cross you and clash with your rage.

–Translated from Tamil by A K Ramanujam

Vijayanagar never rose again. Later kings shifted their capital to the fort at Penugonda and made futile attempts to raise an army. As always there were many rival claimants to the throne, endless intrigue and shifting alliances. Many of the powerful chieftains, the Nayaks, gradually broke free, many of them establishing their own small kingdoms from the remnants of the empire. Among them the more successful Nayaka kings rose at Madura, Thanjavur and Gingee. The last official dynasty of the Karnatak–Vijayanagar Empire was the Aravidu Dynasty but they never ruled from the city of Vijayanagar, however they continued to survive for a century more.

In the middle of the 16th century, the political scene was changing. In the North the Mughals were rising and Akbar was building an empire to rival Vijayanagar. Soon he would eye the five sultanates of South India and ultimately all of them would be absorbed into the Mughal Empire. At the same time new European powers were rising – the Portuguese, French, English and the Dutch would battle for the lucrative trade and ultimately transform themselves into colonial powers. Within a few centuries the last great Hindu Empire of the land would be forgotten.

THE KINGS OF VIJAYANAGAR

Sangama Dynasty	Rest of India
Harihara I 1336–56	
Bukka I 1356–77	Tughlak Dynasty in Delhi
Harihara II 1377–1404	Bahmani Dynasty in Deccan
Virupaksha I 1404–5	
Bukka II 1405–6	
Deva Raya I 1406–22	Sayyid Dynasty in Delhi
Ramachandra 1422	
Vira Vijaya Bukka 1422–24	
Deva Raya II 1424–46	
Mallikarjuna 1446–65	Lodi Dynasty in Delhi
Virupaksha II 1465–85	
Praudha Deva Raya 1485	

Saluva Dynasty	
Saluva Narasimha 1485–91	Five sultanates of Bijapur
Thimma Bhupala 1491	Golconda, Bidar, Berar
Narasimha II 1491–1505	and Ahmednagar in Deccan

Tuluva Dynasty	
Narasa Nayaka 1491–1503	
Vira Narasimha 1503–9	
Krishnadeva Raya 1509–29	1526. First Battle of Panipat.
Achutya Raya 1529–42	Babur and the Mughal Dynasty
Sadashiva 1542–70	Emperor Akbar

THE RAYA AND THE FARMER'S DAUGHTER

Medieval historians and travellers cultivated wonderful gossips, often gathering their information from bazaars and from palace retainers. Mohammad Qasim Ferishta wrote his chronicle *Tarikh-i-Ferishta* in the 17th century during the reign of Jahangir. In it he also included the history of the Bahmani sultans and the Rayas of Vijayanagar even though by then both the kingdoms had vanished; so most of his information came from oral sources and documents and it is a very valuable chronicle as in many cases he had referred to records that have since been lost.

One of the juiciest stories he relates is about how in AD 1406, Deva Raya I came into conflict with Firuz Shah Bahmani over the beautiful daughter of a farmer from Mudkul. Ferishta starts his tale of a lovelorn Raya writing,

> *There resided in the town of Mudkul a farmer, who was blessed with a daughter of such exquisite beauty that the Creator seemed to have united all his powers in making her perfect.*

> *This girl called Pertal was being educated by an old Brahmin who went to Vijayanagar and praised her beauty to the Raya. The king promptly sent him back with rich gifts for Pertal's parents, asking for their daughter's hand.*

Then Ferishta continues,

> *The parents were overjoyed at such unexpected good fortune and calling for the young maid, laid before her the rich gifts of the Raya ... attempted to throw upon her neck a golden collar set with jewels, as a token of immediate espousal... The beautiful virgin, to their great astonishment, drawing her neck from compliance, refused to receive the collar, and observed, that whoever entered the harem of Beejanuggur, was afterwards not permitted to see even her nearest relations and friends; and though they might be happy to sell her for worldly riches, yet she was too fond of her parents to submit to eternal absence from them, even for all the splendour of the palace of Beejanuggur.*

Hearing such loving words the girl's parents changed their minds and sent the Brahmin away. The old man went back to Deva Raya and reported the failure of his mission. Furious at such rejection, the Raya now marched out with an army to forcibly take away the girl. What he forgot in his hurry was that the farmer lived in an area that was disputed between Vijayanagar and the Bahmani kingdoms and that at that time Mudkul was being controlled by Firuz Shah.

When the army arrived at the village they discovered that all the people had fled including Pertal's family. On their way back the troops looted some villages and that was enough provocation for Firuz Shah to declare a new jihad against Vijayanagar. And he was helped in this enterprise by the traditional enemies of the Rayas—the Velamas of Telengana and the Reddis of Rajahmundry.

Firuz invaded Vijayanagar in the winter of AD 1406 and after a few setbacks he occupied the outer areas of the city and laid siege to it. Meanwhile his troops roamed around the countryside looting and taking prisoners. Finally, Deva Raya sued for peace and had to agree to a humiliating treaty in which he paid a huge tribute, lost the fort of Bankapur and had to give a daughter in marriage to Firuz. Some modern historians question this marriage as no contemporary source mentions it but interestingly Ferishta has even given a detailed description of the wedding celebrations that followed.

As he writes,

For forty days communication was open between the city and the Sultan's camp. Both sides of the road were lined with shops and booths, in which the jugglers, drolls, dancers and mimic of Carnatic displayed their feats and skill to amuse travellers. The Khankhanan and Meer Fuzzul Oollah (Bahmani noblemen), with the customary presents of a bridegroom, went to Beejanuggur from whence ... they brought back the bride.

Deva Raya invited his new son-in-law to visit him and he and his bride proceeded to Beejanuggur ... the road was spread with cloth of gold, velvet, satin and other rich stuff. The two princes rode on horseback together, between ranks of beautiful boys and girls, who waved plates of gold and silver flowers over their heads as they advanced, and then threw them to be gathered by the populace ... upon their arrival at the palace gate, (they) ascended a splendid palanquin, set with valuable jewels, in which they were carried together to the apartments.

According to Ferishta, Firuz stayed in Vijayanagar for three days before returning to Gulbarga. Sadly, history teaches us that old enemies usually remain enemies. Firuz decided that he had been insulted by Deva Raya because the Raya had not come to bid him a formal goodbye and vowed, 'one day (to) have his revenge for the affront offered him by such neglect'. So hostilities between the two kingdoms were renewed soon enough.

What happened to the beautiful Pertal whose rejection of the Raya started it all? According to Ferishta, the Sultan had brought her to Gulbarga and married her off to his eldest son Hasan Khan, who according to Ferishta was 'a weak and dissipated prince ... entirely devoted to indolence and pleasure'. All we know is that Hasan never became the sultan. As for that unnamed princess of Vijayanagar carried away as a silent pawn in her father's political games, she vanished into the sultan's harem and was soon forgotten.

It was a familiar fate for medieval princesses and farmers' pretty daughters.

Chapter Four

KRISHNADEVA RAYA

Profile of the greatest monarch of Vijayanagar

His powerful personality, his prowess in war, courage and fearlessness are amply demonstrated by the innumerable campaigns which he led in person in the first half of his rule.

– K Raghavacharlu

4

He did not succeed to a peaceful kingdom or an easy reign. The empire was surrounded by powerful and traditionally inimical rulers waiting for the first opportunity to invade. Within his realm there were rebellious feudal lords who still resented the Tuluva Dynasty's ascendancy and regularly raised the standard of rebellion. During the last period of internal troubles large stretches of land had been annexed by other kings and had to be recovered. Finally, there was a huge empire with its myriad problems that had to be administered with a firm but kind hand.

Krishnadeva Raya faced all these challenges and still had the time to patronise the arts, compose poetry, build a new city, new temples, order the creation of sacred images and *gopurams* in Vijayanagar. Most importantly, he won a rare period of peace and prosperity for his people through his success in the battlefield that allowed Vijayanagar to reach its zenith in prosperity and richness of culture.

The Sangam poet Kappiyaru Kapiyanar has written about another king,

Blood glows like the sky before nightfall
in the red centre of the battlefield.

These finely carved 'musical pillars' of the Vitthala Temple are one of the most popular tourist attractions. When beaten by the local guides with wooden sticks, they emit different notes.

Facing page: *The broken plinth of a vanished temple near Vitthala showing carvings of Lord Krishna, Narasimha and prancing horses.*

Following page right and left: *Ruined figures of Krishnadeva Raya and one of his queens, which can be seen at the Kamalapura Archaeological Museum.*

Pages 108–09: *A balustrade shaped like an uncoiled snake.*

Demons dance there.
And your kingdom is an unfailing harvest
Of victorious wars.

–Translated from Tamil by A K Ramanujam

A Many-Hued Monarch...

Krishnadeva Raya's reputation as the most illustrious of the kings of the Vijayanagar Empire begins in the battlefield. This was a kingdom that was always at war and it was in the battlefield that he proved his mettle. He knew that it was only with military

Intricate carvings of animals, birds, demons and mythical creatures that showcase the visual imagination of the sculptors.

dominance that he could bring peace and prosperity to his people and he achieved this with decisive success.

What is intriguing is the qualities he shares with another great monarch who would come to power thirteen years after his death—the Mughal emperor Jalaluddin Akbar. They were men of complex, many-faceted and vivid qualities. As warriors and generals both men remained undefeated in the battlefield. As rulers they were efficient administrators; they exhibited an enlightened spirit of tolerance and genuine love for art and culture. Both of them were great builders and just as Akbar left the magical city of Fatehpur Sikri for posterity, Krishnadeva's temples and palaces still stand among the ruins of Hampi and amaze visitors with their elegance of design.

On the battlefield, Krishnadeva always led his forces from the front and inspired his men with his reckless courage. Stories of his acts of valour and presence of mind became the stuff of legends that minstrels sang about in temple courtyards. He was an inventive military strategist facing every challenge with highly original solutions. His royal standard with the symbol of the boar flew in triumph over the capitals of all his enemies—Cuttack, Gulbarga, Bijapur and Bidar. He was ruthless during battle but

never sacked a conquered city or ordered the massacre of a defeated army. As a true leader, he knew the right gestures of generosity that won him the loyalty of his men. For instance, after every battle he would move around the battlefield searching for men lying wounded and make sure that they were given help. Like all great generals, he knew his soldiers personally and the best warriors were selected to join elite battalions. These men would fight with ferocious courage and absolute loyalty. He studied the success of his enemies and equipped his army with the best horses, cannons and muskets and even hired Portuguese musketeers.

Krishnadeva was himself a worshipper of Vishnu and built new temples, added *gopuram*s and *mandapa*s in Vijayanagar. He built the Krishnaswamy Temple where he enshrined the

The elephant Lotus Mahal may have been the palace of the king.

image of Balagopal that he brought from Udayagiri and added an ornate hall to the Hazara Rama Temple within the royal complex which was probably his royal chapel. He deeply venerated Lord Venkateshwara-Balaji at Tirupati and there are records of at least three royal visits to the temple. He presented the deity with a jewel-studded crown, a necklace of pearls and silver plates. On later visits he presented a sword decorated with diamonds, rubies and sapphires and after the great victory at Udayagiri he came with his queens and covered the image with thirty thousand gold coins. The standing images of the king and his two queens can still be seen in the first *mandapa* of the Tirupati Temple. However, his personal faith never intruded into his duties as a king. All religions were allowed to flourish freely within the empire; it was ability that won the king's patronage not religion; and he gave religious grants to many sects. As Barbosa writes, 'The king allows such freedom that every man may come and go and live according to his own creed, without suffering any annoyance.'

Krishnadeva's empire was efficiently run and in spite of spending so much time at war, he would go on royal tours every year to meet his subjects and hear their petitions. He was active in improving agriculture with better irrigation systems and took the help of the Portuguese to build canals and water reservoirs, among them was a giant tank in the town of Nagalapura that he built near Vijayanagar. He continued with the tradition of repairing and building of temples and many shrines have *gopuram*s and pillared halls that were built by him. This was the time that the eye-catching *gopuram* gateways began to soar above the temples and came to

Following page: *Each pillar of the Vitthala Temple is a piece of sculpture by itself, with carvings of deities, horses and mythical creatures.*

symbolise South Indian sacred architecture. The first was the *gopuram* at the Virupaksha Temple at Hampi that welcomes pilgrims as it soars at the end of the main arcade of the Hampi Bazaar.

Like many of his predecessors, Krishnadeva Raya was an energetic patron of arts and letters. He honoured eight scholars and poets in Sanskrit, Telugu and Kannada who came to be called the *Ashtadiggaja*s. The premier among them was Allasani Pedanna, the poet laureate who was revered by the king. It is said that Krishnadeva personally tied a gold anklet around Pedanna's feet and lifted his palanquin on his shoulders. There was also his confidant Tenali Ramakrishna Kavi, who was a serious poet but has been remembered more for his sense of humour. Coincidently, just like Tenali Raman, Akbar would have a friend with an anarchic wit in Raja Birbal who was also a poet.

Krishnadeva was himself a good composer of verses and fortunately one of his long poems – *Amukta Malyada* – has survived and has been praised for its literary qualities. In it he has long passages where he describes the duties of a king and reflects an enlightened and compassionate attitude towards his subjects.

Krishnadeva was given many titles like *Andhra Bhoja* (King of the Andhras), *Kannada Rajya Rama Ramana* (Great King of the Kannadas) and *Moorurayaraganda* (King of Three Seas).

A Day in the Life of Krishnadeva...

Reading about this brilliant, complex monarch one wonders about his personality and what he looked like and fortunately Domingo Paes has left a detailed description of Krishnadeva, his personal life and his daily schedule. Reading his words, it is clear that Paes was both fascinated and impressed by the Vijayanagar king. And do remember these words of praise are not being written by a sycophantic royal historian, but a traveller from another land who is taking a critical look at him. As he writes,

> *This king is of medium height and of fair complexion and good figure, rather fat than thin; he has on his face signs of smallpox. He was the most feared and perfect king that could possibly be, cheerful of disposition and very merry; he is one that seeks to honour foreigners and receives them kindly, asking about all their affairs whatever their condition may be. He is a great ruler and a man of much justice, but subject to sudden fits of rage, and this is his title, 'Crisnarao Macagao', King of kings, Lord of the greater lords of India, Lord of the three seas and of the land.*

The word '*macagao*' was probably Paes' version of maharaja. Like all warriors Krishnadeva was also an athlete and enjoyed wrestling and horse riding. According to Paes,

> *The king is accustomed every day to drink a quartilho (three-quarter pints) of oil of gingelly before daylight, and anoints himself all over with the said oil; he covers his loins with a small cloth, and takes in his arms great weights made of earthenware, and then, taking a sword, he exercises himself with it till he has sweated out all the oil, and then he wrestles with one of his wrestlers. After this labour he mounts a horse and gallops about the plain in one direction and another till dawn, for he does all this before day break.*

Then Krishnadeva bathed and the family's Brahmin priest would give him a ceremonial wash. Next he headed to the royal chapel, which may have been the Hazara Rama Temple for his morning puja. Paes mentions that the king liked to wear white silk garments embroidered with 'roses in gold' and wore a collar of diamonds around his neck. He calls this piece of jewellery a 'pateca' or the pattika which was a strip of cloth embellished with precious stones and pearls that was very popular at that time. As his images show, he wore a high conical cap 'of brocade in fashion like a Galician helmet, covered with a piece of fine stuff all of fine silk'.

Thus clad in silks and jewels Krishnadeva would sit in court to listen to reports and petitions, pass judgements and give orders. His audience chamber was an open pillared hall, a *mandapa* that the Vijayanagar kings favoured and built at many places. The pillars were intricately carved and Paes mentions two stone images of women at

Facing page: *The* maha mandapa *of the Vitthala Temple built by King Krishnadeva Raya is the finest example of the sacred architecture of the Vijayanagar Empire.*

An aged and graceful frangipani tree in the courtyard of the Vitthala Temple.

the entrance, and the chamber had brightly painted walls. Saluva Timma would be in attendance to guide the proceedings and Paes comments that 'he commands the whole household and to him all the great lords act as to the king'.

Paes attended some of these proceedings and describes the etiquette at the royal court. The noblemen would enter doing a namaskar where they raised their hands above their heads and then would stand in rows against the sides. They stood all through the proceedings, in complete silence, with their hands tucked into the sleeves of their robes, their eyes lowered and no one chewed betel before the king. As a matter of fact it was considered a great honour if the king shared a betel with anyone. It was only when the king addressed any nobleman that he raised his head and replied to the king's question. At the end of the audience, they all left after another elaborate round of namaskars.

Paes was present at one such audience when Krishnadeva honoured the Portuguese soldier Christovao de Figueiredo and his musketeers who played such a crucial role in the siege of Raichur Fort. He writes,

> *The king gave him… a* cabaya *(robe) of brocade with a cape of the same fashion as the king wore, and to each one of the Portuguese he gave a cloth embroidered with many pretty figures and the king gives this because it's customary; he gives it in token of friendship and love.*

Paes says that Krishnadeva had twelve lawful wives of which three were principal ones. However inscriptions of his time only mention two queens—Chinna Devi and Tirumale Devi.

The latter was from the royal family of Seringapattanam, a vassal of Vijayanagar and was given the title of *Pattada Rani*, principal queen. The image of himself and his two queens that Krishnadeva donated to the Tirupati shrine also has Tirumale standing on his right as the chief queen. Krishnadeva also married an Oriya princess whose name was probably Jaganmohini (*See* Box).

Scenes from a royal procession carved on the plinth of a mandapa *in the Vitthala Temple.*

Paes mentions a courtesan who was Krishnadeva's mistress when he was a young prince and she made him promise that he would make her queen if he ever won the throne. He kept his promise and married her. Paes claims that he built the town called Nagalapura and named it after this courtesan but in fact, his mother's name was Nagambika and it was probably dedicated to the queen mother. Krishnadeva was survived by two daughters Tirumalamba and Vengalamba, one of whom was married to Rama Raya who would play a crucial role in the history of Vijayanagar after the reign of Krishnadeva Raya.

Warrior, statesman, poet, builder and enlightened king—Krishnadeva Raya was a complete monarch.

A PRINCE AND PRINCESS FROM ORISSA

Battles are not just about acts of bravery and cowardice, there are stories of lives that get drawn into the vortex of war and are changed forever. These tragedies remain in the memory of people and get transformed into legends.

One such legend is about the two children of Prataparudra, the Gajapati of Orissa. When Krishnadeva captured the Udayagiri Fort, among the prisoners were Prince Virabhadra, son and heir to the Kalinga throne and one of Prataparudra's queens. Krishnadeva sent them to Vijayanagar where, according to contemporary literature, they were treated with courtesy as guests of the royal family. However, Virabhadra is said to have committed suicide and Fernao Nuniz tells an incredible tale of why the prince killed himself.

According to Nuniz, Krishnadeva had heard that Virabhadra was 'very dextrous with both sword and dagger, and he would be pleased to see him fence'. Next day, the king had his best sword fighter ready to fence with the prince. In Nuniz's words,

> *When the son of the King of Orya saw him, being offended with the King for sending a man to fight with him who was not the son of a King but only a man of humble birth, he cried out to the King, 'God forbid that I should soil my hands by touching a man not of the royal blood'. And saying this he slew himself.*

The story was probably bazaar gossip as historians doubt the veracity of this rather colourful tale as there is epigraphic evidence that at a later date, Virbhadra was acting as the governor of a province.

The Gajapati agreed to give a daughter in marriage in return for his queen and Krishnadeva also returned some of the land that he had conquered. This Oriya princess was called Jaganmohini or Tuka. Tradition says that some years earlier the Gajapati had carried off a princess of Vijayanagar, so by asking for her hand Krishnadeva was sort of returning the courtesy. Clearly Tuka was not happy with the arrangement because she tried to poison the king and Krishnadeva was only saved by the timely intervention of Saluva Timma. Tuka was banished from Vijayanagar and sent off to live in Kambham. Later, she seemed to have regretted her action and wrote five Sanskrit verses known as *Tukapancaka*, where she expresses repentance and begs for her lord's forgiveness. Again Saluva Timma entered the scene as he interceded on her behalf and she was reconciled with the king and allowed to return to the royal harem.

Chapter Five

LIVING IN VIJAYANAGAR

Recreating the life of the people

Contemporary texts delight in giving details of elaborate banquets with innumerable delicious dishes, entertainments with music and theatrical performances, and picnics and hunting expeditions on the outskirts of the city.

– John M Fritz and George Michell

5

It is easy to find a hill to climb in Hampi, the low ridges and piled boulders are everywhere. There are two hills—Matanga and Hemkuta—at the two ends of the Hampi Bazaar that no one can miss. When you clamber up to the rocky summit of Matanga Parvatam, pause and look around to get an unparalleled view of the ruins of Vijayanagar. Then pause for a while, open all the windows of your mind, and recreate a living city in the landscape before you.

It is a panorama that you will never forget, as it is like none other anywhere in the world. On the right is the broad arcade of the Hampi Bazaar with the stone cubicles where they once sold flowers, fruits and incense, silks, cottons, copper plates and bowls—all that you took to offer to Lord Virupaksha at his ancient shrine down the road. Right below is the giant Nandi bull that has sat here with stoic patience for centuries serenely accepting the worship of pilgrims. On the left, straight below the hill is Achyut Raya's Tiruvengalanatha Temple and from your eagle-eyed view you can see its hoary granite walls and spires nestling among the palm and betel trees. Looking at this sleepy, semi-rural scene it is hard to imagine that once the Hampi Bazaar was a cosmopolitan place teeming with traders who

Village girls at Kamalapuram who live among the ruins of palaces.

Facing page: *Worshipping Surya, the Sun God and Pampa, the River Goddess with the chanting of mantras.*

A stage at the end of the Bazaar hosts performances at the annual Hampi festival.

Pages 126–27: *The ancient ghats by the Tungabhadra that have seen pilgrims from a time before the rise of Vijayanagar.*

came from distant lands—Arabs, Jews, Persians, Chinese, Malay, Portuguese and Parsis.

Turn around and you'll see that huge ochre, pink-streaked grey granite boulders are scattered everywhere; often piled precariously to form teetering hills, and through this barren, forbidding landscape the sparkling waters of the Tungabhadra meander and cascade like a playful ribbon. There has been human habitation here for at least three thousand years but what put it on the map of history was the foundation of Vijayanagar. Everywhere you look, you'll see the exquisite but ruined buildings – temples, palaces, pavilions and

bazaars – all built of that mellow red-gold stone, the colour of the vermilion we smear across the forehead of a dark goddess. And as you stand there you try to imagine what the life of the people of this magnificent city must have been like over six centuries ago.

During the time of Krishnadeva Raya, Vijayanagar was the most famous city in India, rivalling Delhi in splendour. Travellers, traders and adventurers arrived from distant lands and in the chronicles they left behind we find portraits of unsurpassed grandeur and courtly elegance and it was the royal family that set the tone of this opulence and luxury. Abdur Razzaq, the envoy from the court of Sultan Shahrukh of Persia, wrote in AD 1444, 'The city of Bidjanagar is such that the pupil of the eye has never seen a place like it, and the ear of intelligence has never been informed that there existed anything to equal it in the world.'

A family of pilgrims take a breather by the Tungabhadra River.

A watchtower looms over the ruins of palaces.

The city was divided into two clearly demarcated zones—the temple enclosure and the royal enclave. The great Virupaksha Temple stands at the heart of the sacred temple zone with a broad avenue leading off from its main gateway. There are arcades of shops on both sides of the avenue – this was the famous Hampi Bazaar that amazed visitors. The rich in Vijayanagar were a cosmopolitan lot with highly selective tastes in fine products. The shops here sold gold and precious stones, the finest cotton and silk, carvings in stone and wood, pottery, metal ware, spices and perfumes. Also there were inns and food shops, homes of noblemen and courtesans. Contemporary literature talks of shops selling flower garlands and betel shops managed by pert, flirtatious *paanwalis*.

The Arabs and Portuguese traders came to sell velvets, brocades and horses; the Chinese brought porcelain and silks; the Roman traders came bearing amphorae of wines and they headed back with sacks of aromatic spices and muslin as gossamer as spider's web. The famous Chinese general Cheng Ho may have been here as he made seven voyages across the Indian Ocean during the reign of the Ming Dynasty in the 15th century and visited many South Indian ports.

A watchtower in the zenana *area.*

The Royal Life...

The lifestyle of the nobility was always an imitation of the way the royal family lived. The Royal Enclosure was separated from the city by high walls with octagonal watchtowers. Within were separate areas for the king and his women. The women's palaces in the *zenana* area were enclosed by another high wall with watchtowers for female guards. Inside were stately and elegant palaces and bathing pools set within orchards and gardens. Among the palaces the most attractive is the two-storied pillared pavilion called Lotus Mahal. It has arched doorways and airy windows leading into intimate rooms that must have been luxuriously furnished with soft carpets and low divans, brass lamps hanging from the brackets on the top of the pillars glimmering with golden tips of light, brocade cushions and bolsters, silk curtains and incense smoking in copper bowls.

Even now, when it is just bare walls and dilapidated pillars, the palace has a flirtatious, feminine air of warmth and welcome. This was the king's private world—of queens, princesses, concubines and courtesans. Here he not only came to enjoy the company of royal women but also for the knowledge and advice of the older queens and princesses, who were often influential women. The *zenana* was where he held his most confidential meetings and conferred with spies and ministers. One can imagine the king coming here after a hard day's work to relax as the women sang, played the veena and the air echoed to the jangle of ankle bells as they danced for him. South Indian literature always depicts kings as being surrounded by adoring women. As George Michell comments, 'in this respect, he is conceived as an irresistible erotic figure'.

In the royal zone there are pools and baths for royalty to frolic in and the prettiest is the Queen's Bath—a water pavilion of truly delightful architectural design. It has a rather deceptively plain exterior but when one walks into the arcaded corridor surrounding the pool, a world of sensuous playfulness opens out before the visitor. Ornate little alcoves look over the pool and the roof is arched and covered in delicate stucco patterns. One can imagine the sun streaming in through the latticed windows to take a peek at the joyful scene inside – the women splashing in the water, drying their hair in the overhanging balconies, doing their make-up by a window, as the walls echoed to their chatter and laughter.

The royal men lived in more majestic palaces next to the royal family shrine, the Hazara Rama Temple. All that remains of these palaces are the many-tiered stone platforms covered with carved panels that are like a moving panorama of the life in Vijayanagar. Here we have it all carved in stone – the marching soldiers holding spears and swords, the dancing women with flared skirts, horses and elephants with elaborate saddles and

Facing page: *Once a pavilion in Vijayanagar, this structure has been transformed into a village home.*

The intricately carved enclosure wall of the Hazara Rama Temple.

howdahs, drummers, flute players, jesters and occasionally, European men in tilting hats and a row of camels with benign smiles on their craggy faces. The palaces were all built of wood, stucco and bricks on these granite platforms and all that remains are the holes where the pillars were placed. In Vijayanagar it was the gods and goddesses who got homes made of lasting stone; the kings built their own palaces with more modest materials.

The description of their sybarite lifestyles does not really do justice to the kings. These were warriors and busy administrators who had to run a large, sprawling empire and had little time to luxuriate in decadent living. If they did, their enemies would invade and take it all away from them. A large part of their lives were spent in military campaigns, living in army camps or on the road, moving in slow

Fertile green paddy fields, dotted with tall coconut palms, which stand elegantly against the rocky terrian.

procession across the landscape. The first decade of Krishnadeva's reign was spent in ceaseless war and when at home his day began before dawn and he would be hard at work till dusk. One wonders when he found the time to compose poetry. It was during festivals that the royal and the spiritual combined to produce a show of dazzling pageantry. The most important celebration of the royal calendar was Mahanavami in autumn when there were nine days of religious rituals, parades, fireworks, feasting, dancing and music. It was not a festival reserved for royalty alone but a carnival for the people and all of Vijayanagar joined in the celebrations. The main ceremony was held at the palace called the Mahanavami Dibba. One of the most detailed descriptions of the festival has been given by Domingo Paes and he calls the palace the House of Victory. (*See* Box).

Varthema describes the magnificent clothes worn by the king. He *wears a cap of gold brocade two spans long, and when he goes to war he wears a quilted dress of cotton, and over it he puts another garment full of golden piastres, and having all around it jewels of various kinds. His horse is worth more than some of our cities, on account of the ornaments which it wears. When he rides for his pleasure he is always accompanied by three or four kings, and many other lords, and five or six thousand horses, wherefore he may be considered to be a very powerful lord.*

Paes writes that the wooden walls of the palace were lined with silk embroidered with seed pearls and rubies and images of lions made of gold were placed at corners. Here the king worshipped the family deity while outside, the musicians played and the *devadasi*s danced.

Rows of horses and elephants in gorgeous trappings lined the avenue and the king came out to worship them by throwing flowers and sprinkling them with incense. As the people watched, the army commanders came marching up to receive honours; there were wrestling matches, javelin and archery contests, horse races and finally fireworks to light up the sky in a million sparkling flames.

The nobility dressed in the finest cotton and silk embroidered with gold thread. Both men and women wore a lot of jewellery and during celebrations the queens were so laden with gold that maids were needed to help them walk! The rich ventured out with a servant holding an elaborate umbrella over them made of silk with gold tassels. They perfumed themselves with sandalwood, aloes, camphor, musk and saffron mixed with rose water. Even the royal animals lived in greater comfort than ordinary people. The royal Elephant Stables were built of granite and had a pretty domed roof and thick-walled stalls, while the poor of the city lived in mud brick and thatched huts.

The economy of the city was centred round the patronage of the rich and the arrival of pilgrims. The king was also the biggest employer of bureaucrats, soldiers, maids, stewards, charioteers, gardeners, cooks…; what is notable is the lack of prejudice in employing people. Many soldiers and even army commanders were Muslims and they were allowed to take their oath of allegiance on the Holy Koran. This was a liberal society and many women were employed in the government; the king's personal guards were women, some even worked as accountants and Paes even mentions female wrestlers! The city was divided into different localities reserved for different crafts that depended on royal patronage. There were weavers, wood and stone carvers, jewellers, potters, metal workers and painters and they all had space allotted to them. Just as they supplied their wares to the royal family, they also provided them to the deities in the temples and to the shops in the bazaars. Here flowers, fruits, vegetables, incense, cloth and food stalls sat next to the cubicles of astrologers, priests and magic potion men.

If you asked the king who was the real royalty in Vijayanagar he would have said it was Lord Virupaksha and his consort Devi Pampa and that he was just their servant on earth. As a matter of fact, they signed all royal edicts in the name of their deity. So the temples were patrons too – not just of craftspeople but also of scholars, musicians, dancers, poets and philosophers. In many ways, the patronage of the temple took precedence over that of the king. Krishnadeva employed stone carvers, architects and labourers to build the main *gopuram* of the Virupaksha Temple. He and his queens took part in elaborate pujas where they would need hundreds of priests. During the chariot festival, the Brahmotsavam and other auspicious occasions, the city would be flooded with pilgrims who would bring good business to the bazaars.

Facing page: *The tallest* gopuram *of the Virupaksha Temple is visible at a curve of the Tungabhadra River.*

At festival time, the temple bazaar overnight turns into a riot of colours, smells and tastes.

When you sit in the *natya mandapa* of the Vitthala Temple imagine a dance recital there, with lamps glowing by the pillars as a dancer flits in and out of the light and shadows before a gorgeously dressed assembly of royalty and nobility. Listen to the raised voices of the singers and the drums keeping beat to the flying hands and feet and the jangle of heavy anklets and beyond it, in the dim, lamp-lit sanctum sanctorum – the remote Godhead's bejewelled eyes watching over them all. Unlike today's ostentatious and empty display of wealth, the lifestyles, ceremonies and celebrations of the rulers of Vijayanagar were not merely for show but were rooted in patronage, cultural pride and religious tradition. Royal pomp and pageantry came with the generosity of sharing and the beauty of classical good taste.

The People and Their Deities...

All the foreign travellers commented on how densely populated the Vijayanagar Empire was and as Abdur Razzaq wrote, 'It is so well populated that it is impossible to give an idea of it.' And the estimate of historians range from fifteen to eighteen million people. There were many important towns and ports like Honawar, Bhatkal, Mangalore, Srisailam, Calicut and Mylapur (which is the oldest section of modern Chennai). Also there were sacred towns like Kanchipuram, Chidambaram and Madurai. The greatest city among them all was of course Vijayanagar, like they said of Rome – all the roads led to it.

The coastal areas were very fertile and one of the main crops was rice. Also wheat, sugarcane, lentils, gingelly, turmeric, ginger, areca nuts and cotton were grown. There were spices, fruits and vegetables

Devotees build auspicious sand lingams *on the banks of the Tungabhadra during festivals.*

both among the loveliest shrines in Hampi. Similarly, Narasimha, the man-lion avatar of Vishnu, was immortalised in the giant statue that even in its ruined state dominates the landscape. Among the goddesses, Kali as Ellamma was very popular and still has a number of living shrines in the city. The images of the Ramayana deities are everywhere, including the walls of the Hazara Rama Temple and the most spectacular are the images of Hanuman as Anjaneya that you see carved on rocks everywhere. They are carved in profile, his long tail curving up above his head, 'one arm raised in defiance', and being a fun-loving deity, at times also holding a bunch of lotus blossoms.

Craftsmen and Merchants...

In matters of crafts and industry, Vijayanagar was more advanced than Europe and the balance of trade was in its favour. Vijayanagar was self-sufficient in most products like textiles, metal ware and even luxury goods and most of the time the royal treasury took payment in gold and used it to buy Arab and Persian horses and elephants from Lanka. Like today, the Andhra and Tamil regions were great centres of cotton and silk weaving, and textiles and spices were the biggest exports westward to Europe and eastward to Malacca and Sumatra. In this way, the Indian woven motifs and printing techniques travelled the world. The chintz that the factories of Manchester began to produce a couple of centuries later was the *chhint* we are familiar with and our endless variety of mango motifs, the *ambi*, became the paisley that became so popular in Europe.

The Portuguese traveller Duarte Barbosa wrote in AD 1501 about the wares on display in Hampi Bazaar,

Following page: *Shops crammed with local handicrafts flank the street leading to the Virupaksha Temple.*

> *Here there is a diamond mine whence are obtained many good diamonds; all other precious stones are brought hither for sale from Pegu (Burma) and Ceilam (Ceylon) and from Ormus they bring pearls… here also is used the brocades… from China and Alexandria also metals both wrought and unwrought, copper in abundance, quick silver, vermilion, saffron, rose water, great stores of opium, sanderswood, aloes-wood, camphor, musk and scented materials. Likewise much pepper is used here, which they bring from Malabar…*

In the early years of the empire, sea trade was a monopoly of the Muslims, mostly Arabs who had settled along the Malabar Coast. However, by the early years of the 16th century, the Portuguese had arrived with their warships and used aggressive fire power to snatch away this trade, so that by Krishnadeva's time most of the sea trade was in Portuguese hands, largely from the port of Goa. Among the exports during his reign were textiles, spices, rice, sugar, iron and saltpetre. Vijayanagar imported horses, elephants, pearls, copper, coral, mercury, vermilion, Chinese silks and Arab velvets. Among the Hindus the most successful trading community were the Chettiyars whose mansions with Burma teak pillars and ceilings still survive in Tamil Nadu.

A Citizen of Vijayanagar…

The kings lived in palaces, the nobility in mansions and the poor had mud brick walls and a thatched roof as shelter. Barbosa viewing the Royal Enclosure wrote of:

great and fair palaces, with many enclosed courts and great houses very well built, within them are wide open spaces, with water tanks in great numbers… in the city as well there are palaces after the same fashion wherein dwell the great lords and governors thereof.

Paes describing the street with houses of the nobility wrote,

from here to the King's palace is all streets and rows of houses, very beautiful, and houses of Captains and other rich and honourable men; you will see rows of houses with many figures and decorations pleasing to look at.

The wide street leading off the Virupaksha Temple that is now called Hampi Bazaar he said was, 'a very beautiful street of very beautiful houses with balconies and arcades'.

The rich wore elaborate garments in cotton and silk. According to Barbosa,

Their men wear certain clothes, a girdle below would very tightly in many folds and short white shirts of cotton or silk or coarse brocade, which are gathered between the thighs but open in front; on their heads, they carry small turbans, and some wear silk or brocade caps, they wear their rough shoes on their feet without stockings. They wear also other large garments thrown over their shoulders like capes.

Vibrant mounds of coloured powder for worshippers at the Virupaksha Temple.

Then he describes the fashionable wear of upper crust women,

> *the women wear white garments of very thin cotton, or silk of bright colours, five yards long; one part of which is girt round them below and the other part they throw over one shoulder and across their breast in such a way that one arm and shoulder remains uncovered... they wear leather shoes well-embroidered in silk; their heads are uncovered and the hair is tightly gathered into a becoming knot on the top of the head.*

Umbrellas were a status symbol and were made of silk, set with semi-precious gems and with lots of gold tassels, and rich men would strut around with a servant carrying one walking behind them.

As it has always been in India, the farmer, weaver and potter; the water-carrier, servant and washerman were living at a barely subsistence level. The peasants faced heavy taxation from the landowners and also the temples that owned large tracts of fertile land. For them their only way of protesting was to abandon the land and migrate to another region. They toiled away in the sun and rain in their patched dhotis, grateful if they had enough to eat for the next few months. For example, in the early 16th century, the peasants of the North Arcot District paid thirty-three kinds of taxes, thirty-two of which were levied by the temple and one by the crown. Efficient and benevolent kings like Krishnadeva took measures to alleviate their sufferings but during times of conflict all they could expect was more deprivation.

The divisions of society into caste was well entrenched by now but it was not so rigid as in later centuries. There were instances of

Brahmin bureaucrats, army commanders and even one Brahmin sculptor, the man who carved the giant monolith Narasimha statue. One of the duties of the king was to uphold the caste system as the foundation of social order. In every aspect of life—homes, food, marriage, religion, the caste rules were supreme, dividing and at times alienating people. As N Sastri says, 'The emphasis was throughout on the performance of duties attaching to one's station rather than on the rights of the individual or the group.' Both in villages and towns the castes lived in separate areas, cities were planned earmarking lanes for weavers and jewellers, Brahmins and soldiers. The untouchables, doing the most menial of tasks, lived beyond the boundaries of every settlement; their living conditions were not even of humans.

A village woman and her child who live among the ruins of a great empire.

Women and Children...

Looking at the high and forbidding walls of the harem one would think it was the queens and princesses who were hidden behind the purdah in Vijayanagar. However, the travellers often talk of royal women appearing in public, so probably it was not that strictly enforced. They were often educated, cultured women, some wrote poetry like Ganga Devi, the wife of Prince Kumara Kampana who composed the Sanskrit poem *Madhura Vijayam* in praise of his military victories. Two

other Vijayanagar queens, Tirumalamba, wife of Rama Raya and Ramabhadramba, wife of Raghunatha also composed poetry in Sanskrit. There are instances of princesses and queens becoming involved in administration like a Chalukyan princess Akkadevi who administered a province and even took part in army sieges.

All the travellers mention women moving about freely and without any veils within the city. Paes describes in detail the royal women and their attendants at the Mahanavami festival and how they were covered in gold jewellery. Even the attendants were clad in gorgeous silks and wearing gold and diamonds. The ones that caught every traveller's attention were the *devadasi*s who danced during the procession and Paes writes in astonishment, 'Who can fitly describe to you the great riches these women carry on their persons?' And then he lists the jewellery, 'Collars of gold with so many diamonds and rubies and pearls, bracelets also on their arms and on their upper arms, girdles below, and of necessity anklets on their feet' (*See* Box).

Women were not just taking up the accepted professions of dancers and musicians but were also active in many other spheres of life. Fernao Nuniz mentions four thousand women living in the palace including maids, guards and cooks. He says women were astrologers and soothsayers and even worked as accountants, 'whose duty it is to write all the affairs of the kingdom and compare their books with the writers outside... judges as well as bailiffs and watchmen who every night guard the palace, and all these are women.'

Ibn Batuta's comments, written in the 1340s, show that unlike later periods, girls were educated; 'I saw in Hanaur thirteen schools for

Facing page: *Street performers dressed as Lord Ram and Hanuman wander around the pilgrim sites of Hampi.*

Following page: *As in all pilgrimages, the caves around Hampi offer a home for sadhus.*

the instruction of girls, and twenty-three for boys, a thing I have not seen anywhere else.' Boys grew up to learn the crafts or professions practised by their families. Schools were run by Brahmins around temples and the curriculum was a basic one of reading, writing, some mathematics, some Sanskrit *shloka*s, and all learnt through mindless memorising. Higher learning, usually limited to the higher castes, included literature, economics, mathematics, philosophy and some laws. Something that has always intrigued is the absence of geography and science in any curriculum during the ancient and medieval periods.

Before you leave Hampi, wander a while around the expanse of the Mahanavami Dibba where the sides are carved with panels showing the people of Vijayanagar. Here you will see a king wearing that distinctive tall cap is worshipping a *Shivalingam* and there the drummers are playing as the *devadasi*s dance, their skirts flaring around them. Soldiers carrying bows and arrows march past as caparisoned horses and elephants move in procession. A king is sitting on his throne with a maid waving a fly whisk over his head as two Muslim envoys bow before him and Central Asian dancers wearing pointed caps and playing flutes dance for him. In today's Hampi, Vijayanagar and its people live on in eternal stone.

THE TEMPLE DANCERS

The tradition of women being dedicated to a temple can be found in all ancient civilisations including Greece and Egypt. In India, the *devadasi*, the handmaiden of god, was married to the deity as a child and became part of a temple establishment. A *devadasi* was supposed to have the highest status in a hierarchy of the temple after the temple priests and their presence was considered essential during religious rituals. They were well educated, especially in Sanskrit, and trained in music and dance. All our classical dances originate in the precincts of temples where the *devadasi*s worshipped their god through their art. Inscription on the walls of the Brihadishwara Temple built in the 10th century by Raja Raja Chola at Thanjavur states that four hundred *devadasi*s were appointed and given an allowance and land.

With the arrival of the Muslims, the *devadasi* tradition gradually vanished from North India but continued in the South till the 20th century. By the 19th century, with the temples losing both power and prestige, there was a steep decline in both their learning and art and many lived in great poverty. As historian P Subramanian writes, 'Those who were attached to the temples received a fixed salary from the temple which of course was too meagre for their maintenance. They were obliged to sell their favours out of necessity and force of circumstances.' Classical dance performances had declined to become the infamous 'nautch' criticised and called immoral by the Europeans.

In Vijayanagar, *devadasi*s were respected for their art and education and welcomed into the palace. Young men of the nobility were sent to them to learn cultured behaviour and they were treated with respect, for example, no one was allowed to chew betel in the presence of the monarch except the *devadasi*s. They took part in all the rituals and danced before the temple chariot as it travelled down the temple avenue during festivals.

There was a hierarchy among the *devadasi*s according to the various duties of a temple – from sweeping and cleaning to stringing garlands being divided among them. Many were dependent on their meagre salaries from the temple but others were independent women, often highly learned with absolute right to their properties. It was a matriarchal system with daughters inheriting their mother's property and so it was the only section of society where the birth of a girl was welcomed.

Many travellers mention *devadasis* who were fabulously rich, lived in mansions and moved around in expensive palanquins. There was no purdah in Vijayanagar, except for the royal women who lived in the *zenana* but then Paes mentions even queens and princesses attending the Mahanavami festival, watching the parade from the audience hall. Till the 20th century many great classical Bharatanatyam dancers and singers of Carnatic music came from the *devadasi* families and they helped to preserve the art.

The *devadasi* system could only survive with the patronage of the royal family and the temples. After the decline of the empire they lost their social standing; temples could not support them; and they were soon reduced to prostitution. This finally led to an outcry and the system of dedicating young girls to temples where they were exploited by men was banned in the 20th century. *Devadasis* were the guardians of Indian classical dance and music and their decline meant that these arts were nearly lost.

Domingo Paes was fascinated by the amount of jewellery worn by the dancers during the Mahanavami parade and gives a detailed list,

> *On the neck with jewels of gold very richly set with many emeralds and diamonds and rubies and pearls; and besides these many strings of pearls and others for shoulder-belts; on the lower part of the arms many bracelets... on the waist many girdles of gold.*

So he goes on, finally commenting with amusement, 'So great is the weight of the bracelets and gold and jewels carried by them that many of them cannot support them, and women accompany them assisting them by supporting their arms.'

Chapter Six

PILGRIMS BY A SACRED RIVER

The art and architecture of the temples of Hampi

All the pillars of the Parthenon are identical, while no two facets of the Indian temple are the same; every convolution of every scroll is different. No two canopies in the whole building are alike, and every part exhibits a joyous exuberance of fancy, scorning every mechanical restraint. All that is wild in human faith and warm in human feeling is found portrayed on these walls.

– James Fergusson

6

The pilgrim's trail in Hampi begins at the Hemkuta Hill that looms at one end of the Hampi Bazaar, slightly behind the Virupaksha Temple. From here the sacred space spreads out to the two banks of the Tungabhadra River that flows just beyond this main avenue of Hampi, the pilgrim town.

Once this was the spiritual heart of the Vijayanagar Empire and the air seems to still resonate with the echo of temple bells, the chanting of mantras, the mellow aroma of incense and the accumulated prayers of centuries of pilgrims. Here the temporal kings and queens came barefoot to worship at the feet of the Lord of the Universe, God Shiva-Virupaksha and his celestial consort the River Goddess Parvati-Pampa. The divine couple have reigned here from at least the 10th century, much before the time of Vijayanagar and do so till today. Vijayanagar was forgotten for many centuries but Virupaksha's sacred and eternal realm remained vibrantly alive.

This area is scattered with myriad large temples filled with pilgrims, small shrines where only the local people worship and many ruins where the sanctums are empty and silent. Most of the

Details of the carvings at the Pattabhirama Temple.

Facing page: *The illuminated* gopuram *of the Virupaksha Temple. It is the oldest living shrine of Pampakshetra that traces its myths to the Ramayana.*

important Shaiva shrines are to be found around the Hampi village; the Vaishnava temples are located closer to the river and the Jain ones in the south-eastern parts of the city. Many of these religious structures date back to the 9th and 10th centuries, much before Harihara and Bukka arrived at the scene.

Most of the pre-Vijayanagar structures can be found around the ancient village of Hampi and its main shrine of Virupaksha. The older temples are simpler and much smaller creations and it is during the Vijayanagar period that the style bloomed into exuberant and florid carvings.

These later monuments reflect a change in the mindset of the people as archaeologist Percy Brown wrote, 'the country gradually became enriched with buildings in a style showing that the people had been aroused to a life of greater fullness and one which moved them to express with marked freedom and fluency their aesthetic aspirations.'

So a careful study of temples built before and during the Vijayanagar period show the evolution of temple design during this crucial time when sacred architecture took a leap of astonishing creativity. This was achieved with the patronage of the kings of Vijayanagar. The newer elements of design introduced here would influence temple architecture all across South India in the following centuries. The temple motifs that for us epitomise the South Indian, Dravidian style – the open pillared halls called *mandapa*s, the vibrantly carved and highly ornate pillars and the soaring gateways called *gopuram*s – are all gifts of the anonymous architects and sculptors of Vijayanagar.

Pages 156–57: *Every temple precinct has open pavilions for pilgrms.*

Sacred Architecture...

For visitors wandering through these exquisite buildings, some knowledge of the basic design elements of the temples would add much to their visual pleasures. Hindu temples are constructed according to the rules laid down in the ancient Sanskrit canons of architecture and sculpture—the *Vastupurusha Mandala* or *Vastu Shastra*, the *Brihat Samhita* and the *Shilpa Shastra*. In the *Vastu Shastra* the basic rules of sacred architecture were laid down that are followed even today and as historian A L Basham describes them, these *shastra*s are 'an intricate maze of the laws of astronomy,

In Vijayanagar, gopurams *were built with a stone base and a superstructure in brick and plaster, with every surface teeming with images.*

astrology and mathematics to support its codes of architecture.' For example, a temple's main sanctum will always face the east, so that every morning, the first rays of the rising sun can touch the feet of the deity in worship. In the *shastra*s, everything is precisely specified – the placing of the gates along the surrounding walls, the number of doors and windows, the situation of hallways and the spires and pillars.

Similarly, the *Shilpa Shastra* laid down the canons of sculpture and painting. Traditional Indian art prefers the perfect and ideal to the realistic image, so the figures are always very stylised and placed in lyrical postures. Both gods and humans are richly clad with intricate hairstyles and wearing loads of jewellery. The goddesses and the nymphs have sinuous arms and waists, generous breasts and exquisite features. The proportions of the figures are laid down too as gods and goddesses have to be portraits of absolute perfection. As Stella Kramrisch notes about the precision of the canons, 'The height from the soles of the feet up to the root of the hair of the forehead is equal to the width between the tips of the middle fingers when the arms are stretched horizontally.'

One would think that the rigid rules of the *shastra*s would have stifled the creativity of the architects and sculptors but it did not do so. There was always enough leeway to show one's imagination and creative genius and it is amazing how these anonymous and long forgotten craftsmen did not let these canons inhibit their exuberant creativity. A L Basham marvel at the 'delight in the world as the artist found it, a sensual vitality and a feeling of growth and movement as regular and organic as the growth of living things on earth.' As he

Following page: *The exterior walls of the Hazara Rama Temple depict excellent relief sculptures like this portrait of a young and playful Krishna.*

perceptively notes, 'Let it not be thought that Hinduism is morbid, gloomy or forbidding. It is fundamentally a cheerful religion.' This cheerful, exuberant, joy in every aspect of life can be seen in the sculptures all across Hampi, carved on walls, pillars, ceilings and even stray rocks as if the artists could not contain their burgeoning imaginations.

They created temples that were a symbol of heaven on earth covering their outer walls and pillars with myriad deities, dancing nymphs, warriors and mythical beasts, in an uninhibited celebration of every mood of life. Looking closely at these images, what comes through most clearly is the joy they get from their creations and so even while carving ferocious demons and angry beasts there is a sort of vivacity to their work. Even with darker subjects there is nothing gloomy or gothic about the carvings and even an emaciated and wild-haired ascetic will often look quite at peace with his world. Going back to Basham, one of the most sensitive students of Indian art, 'the usual inspiration of Indian art is not so much a ceaseless quest for the Absolute as a delight in the world as the artist found it, a sensual vitality, and a

feeling of growth and movement as regular and organic as the growth of living things on earth.'

During the Vijayanagar period, newer embellishments created temples that became more products of sculpture than architecture in a style that evolved from the earlier Pandya and Chalukyan schools. As the archaeologist D Devakunjari notes in the Archaeological Survey of India handbook, the Vijayanagar style of sacred architecture can be considered a separate category. It is, 'ornate and magnificently exuberant (but) it was not cloyingly florid like the later Chalukyan and Hoysala schools.' There were the highly decorative pillars and ceilings, the intricately designed hallways and subsidiary shrines and the most eye-catching of all, the giant pyramidal *gopuram* gateways covered with vibrant carvings that dominate the landscape and have come to symbolise the temples of the South.

The traditions of temple architecture that evolved at Vijayanagar would be carried on by the Nayaka kings in towns like Vellore, Kumbakonam, Kanchipuram, Chidambaram, Madurai and Srirangam. At Kanchipuram you can see the *mandapa*s at the Varadaraja and Ekambaranatha temples that are in the Vijayanagar style. All the elements that we now know as the Dravidian style of traditional Hindu architecture reached its zenith of creativity during the Vijayanagar Empire.

A Chariot of the Gods...

A temple is a *mandala*, a symbol of the cosmos. In India, monarchs have ruled through the blessings of the pantheon of gods and goddesses and so when they built temples they built them to last, in eternal stone. Temples were always symbols of the power of a king and this was so also at Vijayanagar. Here the temples have lasted because they were built in granite while most of the palaces only had stone basements that survive while their superstructures of brick and wood have vanished long ago.

The heart of any temple is the sanctum sanctorum called the *garbha griha*, the shrine room or the womb house where the main icon is kept. It is a bare, square cell that is kept undecorated, with plain walls so that the focus is completely on the deity standing there at the centre, clad in silks and gold, wreathed in incense smoke and glowing in the light of the tall oil lamps. At the three cardinal points of the outside walls of the sanctum are niches where images of the various aspects of the deity are placed. For example, in a Shiva shrine, the south wall may have the image of the god as a teacher called Shiva Dakshinamurti, the god who faces south. A Vishnu temple will have his avatars like Krishna and Ram. The sanctum is surrounded by a circular corridor used to circle the deity, a part of the Hindu ritual of worship, and this is the *pradakshina patha*.

The *garbha griha* is always crowned by a tall tower or spire called the *shikhara*. The complete unit of the sanctum and its tower is called the *vimana*. The word *vimana* means a chariot or vehicle of the gods and that is why the spire often flies a triumphant flag. The simplest

Facing page: *A pavilion overlooking the Krishna Temple tank.*

Floridly carved pillars and balustrades typical of Vijayanagar.

design of a temple will thus have a *vimana* and a small vestibule before it called the *antarala*. Then as religious rituals became more elaborate, an open pillared hall was attached to the *antarala* called the *mandapa*, facing the door of the sanctum. This was the place where worshippers gathered to watch the various pujas and *arati*s in the *garbha griha*. Over the centuries, the design of the *garbha griha* has changed little as craftsmen have not touched the spiritual heart of the shrine. However the *mandapa* has become more and more elaborate and embellished with sculptures and the greatest creative surge in *mandapa* design took place at Vijayanagar.

The main pillared hall next to the sanctum is called the *maha mandapa* and one of the finest in Hampi is the one at the Vitthala

A beautifully carved elephant balustrade leading to a ceremonial structure in the Royal Enclosure.

Temple with its captivating carved pillars and ceilings. Sometimes there is a small porch leading to the main audience hall, called the *ardha mandapa*, often with elaborate elephant-shaped balustrades. At that time all the temples had *devadasis*, the temple dancers who dedicated their lives to the deity, and they danced and sang in the *natya mandapa* or the *ranga mandapa*. The *bhoga mandapa*, often with a kitchen attached, was where offerings of food were made to the deity during the *yagya* ceremonies and afterwards the pilgrims were fed this consecrated food called *prasad*.

By the 14th century one of the most popular spiritual movements was of Bhakti where the deities were worshipped through personal prayers by their devotees. Some of the greatest sacred poetry was composed by the Bhakti saints of the South like Basavanna and Mahadevi Akka. For them their god was not a remote and judgemental deity but more a friend and guide, a sacred presence they spoke to directly, without the intervention of priests. For Mahadevi, Lord Shiva was her Lord of the Jasmines who spoke to her and listened to her prayers and Basavanna called him Lord of the Meeting Rivers. One

Top: *Pillars at the Pattabhirama Temple exhibit the Vijayanagar style of sculpture.*

Left: *Many temples have carved images of a doorman, a* dvarapala *at their gates.*

of the results of this was that the rituals of worship in temples began to include the verses of the poets and new shrines came up in the temple precinct to various deities and each got their own *mandapa*.

The largest of these shrines was to the consort of the deity and is called the *amman* shrine and they were placed north-west of the main sanctum and slightly behind it. So a Shiva temple got a subsidiary shrine to an aspect of Goddess Parvati, Lord Vishnu to Goddess Lakshmi, and so on. Then a new festival began, where every year, the god and goddess were carried out in a joyous procession in the temple chariot car, the *ratha*, and then married according to the *kalyana* ceremony. So a hall was built for that and attached to the *amman* shrine called the *kalyana mandapa* with brightly painted ceilings and a raised platform in the centre where the icons were placed for the rituals. These *kalyana mandapa*s are some of the most elaborate and at times floridly designed halls in a temple complex.

The most inventive and eye-catching sculptural element in Vijayanagar temples are the pillars that are like individual pieces of art and Percy Brown writes, 'Each becomes a figurative drama in stone'. Even though carved from inert stone, every pillar teems with figures and movement that is nearly fluid with activity. There are the rearing figures of a mythical animal called a *yali* or prancing horses and majestic elephants with riders and other human and demonic figures. Other pillars are transformed into galleries showing the various aspects of the deities, dancing women, warriors and jesters. The tops of the pillars are carved in corbels with pendants and floral motifs. At times the central part is divided into slender columnettes that create a feeling of delicate movement in stone that Brown describes lyrically as 'encircling the central column, a cluster of miniature pillars, slender, mystical and dreamy'. Some of the most intricately carved pillars can be seen at the Vitthalaswami and Krishnaswami temples.

One should not forget that Vijayanagar was often at war and as Hindu temples were known to hold treasures, they were the first places that invaders attacked and looted. As a result, during medieval times, temples were surrounded by high stone walls, creating open courtyards called *prakara*s. Later temples would be encircled by many layers of walls with entrances through a row of gateways of gradually diminishing height. The walls were pierced at the four cardinal directions by entrances and over them the amazing *gopuram* gateways began to soar to the sky. It was in Hampi that the first *gopuram*s were built and they are elegant structures of medium height and quite simply decorated with floral and geometric motifs. The giant *gopuram*s that we are all familiar with, seething with images of gods, demons and humans, painted in dazzling neon colours like giant cinema posters in the sky, would be built in later centuries.

The monuments at Hampi are primarily of two kinds – religious and royal, as the homes of the ordinary people made of bricks and thatch did not survive. Most of the important temples and bazaars are

Facing page: *The magnificent* maha mandapa *within the Pattabhirama Temple. It is the largest temple precinct in Hampi.*

clustered around the banks of the Tungabhadra, with the Virupaksha Temple at the centre of the temple enclosure. The royal citadel with the ruins of palaces, the harem complex called the *zenana*, bathing pools, the royal chapel and various ceremonial structures are in a separate area. The drive from the nearest town of Hospet winds up a hill and then at a curve on top the road divides, the one going downhill to the left leads to the religious enclosure and the other weaving to the right, going past the Krishna Temple and the Narasimha statue, leads to the citadel of the royals of Vijayangar.

The Sacred Zone....

The rich will make temples for Siva
What shall I, a poor man do?
My legs are pillars.
The body the shrine,
The head a cupola of gold.
Listen, O Lord of the Meeting Rivers
Things standing shall fall,
But the moving ever shall stay.

– Basavanna, translated from Kannada by A K Ramanujam

Temples can be found in every corner of Hampi, most of them just a pile of collapsed pillars, others with empty hallways and many of them cannot even be identified as the icons have vanished from the sanctums. Here, only the most architecturally or historically significant temples are being covered as exploring more would take much longer than a single visit to Hampi.

Virupaksha Temple...

No one really knows for sure for how long the shrine of Virupaksha, standing at the bottom of the Hemkuta Hill, has existed in Hampi but if we go by the inscriptions within the precinct, probably from sometime in the 9th or 10th century. So for at least a millennium, its reigning deity Lord Shiva-Virupaksha-Pampapati has received uninterrupted worship from people and it is vibrantly active till today. This is a sacred land and pilgrims gather here in thousands during festivals. The main deities are Lord Virupaksha, an aspect of Shiva and his two consorts the River Goddess Pampa and Goddess Bhuvaneshwari. Hampi Bazaar, the broadest avenue of Vijayanagar, begins at the main, eastern *gopuram* gateway of the temple and ends at the Matanga Hill which stands at the edge of the Tungabhadra River.

One of the names of the Tungabhadra River is Pampa Nadi and the temple celebrates the marriage of Pampa and Lord Shiva, called Virupaksha – the God with Oblique Eyes. So here he is often called Pampapati and the area Pampakshetra or Pampa Tirtha – the pilgrimage of Pampa and Shiva. The Kannada name of Hampi is 'Hampe' a distortion of Pampa. It is said that the goddess performed severe penance to win the hand of Virupaksha who came down to earth and showered the Hemkuta Hill with gold. This celestial marriage is still celebrated every year during the Brahmotsavam festival when the images of the divine couple are taken

A view of the Matanga Hill.

out in a procession down the Hampi Bazaar. At one time the temple dancers used to lead the procession, today as pilgrims crowd the avenue, the drummers and flute players march and play before the rolling wooden chariot car.

The temple complex is a long, rectangular enclosure divided into two *prakara*s. One enters through an imposing eastern *gopuram* gateway that rises to a height of fifty-two metres. It's a white pyramidal tower of nine storeys, gleaming in the sun and it is the first structure that the visitors notice when they look down at Hampi from the road curving down from the hill. Literary evidence says that it was built by Proluganti Tippa, a minister of Deva Raya II (1424–46) and repaired by Krishnadeva Raya in AD 1510. It has the typical *gopuram* design of a two-storey granite base and entrance, over which the brick and plaster tower has been constructed. Unlike the multicoloured *gopuram*s that we see in modern South Indian temples, the stucco design is simple and symmetrical, each storey divided into pilastered niches and topped by a barrel-vaulted roof.

The first *gopuram* leads into an outer courtyard with a smaller *gopuram* at the other end that leads into the central court where the sanctum stands. This smaller *gopuram* was built by Krishnadeva at his coronation in AD 1510 and is in the authentic Vijayanagar style. It is rather square in shape and with three storeys of not much height. He also built a *mandapa*, a 100-pillared hall called *phalapuja mandapa* that stands in the left corner and welcomes weary pilgrims to rest.

Take a breather by the carved pillars of this *mandapa* and watch the world go by. The scene in this courtyard is an eternal one and has not changed much in the centuries. It is always busy with pilgrims and sightseers and filled with movement and happy voices. Women in brilliantly coloured saris with bright orange flowers in their hair go past, excited children run about, vendors call out as they sell fruits and sweets and priests weave in and out of the milling crowd chanting mantras and waving incense to purify the air. From here worshippers now prepare for their main puja by walking barefoot under Krishnadeva's *gopuram* and into the inner *prakara* carrying their offerings in baskets or copper plates.

The innermost enclosure is surrounded by a colonnaded corridor and in the middle stands a tall lamp-stand, a *deepa sthambha*, where hundreds of lamps are lit during religious ceremonies. A stone Nandi bull, Shiva's favourite vehicle sits patiently in the courtyard facing the temple. The sanctum, the *garbha griha*, and its main audience hall, the *maha mandapa*, stand at the other end of the court. This hall was also built by Krishnadeva and as the inscription at the door says, it was built to celebrate his coronation. So it is the earliest example of the florid sculptural style that was developed during his reign. On the composite pillars you see the fantastic, mythical lion-like animal called *yali*, as also a *makara*, a stylised crocodile, elephants and horses along with deities, soldiers and dancing girls. The *yali*s form the main sculptural motif of the pillar and at times have riders

Facing page: *The ruined* gopuram *of the Krishna Temple that was built by King Krishnadeva Raya.*

Pages 174–75: *The stone shrines on Hemkuta Hill are among the oldest in Hampi and were built in the earliest years of the Vijayanagar Empire.*

on their backs as they rear up on their hind legs with prominent eyes and bared fangs.

The most interesting thing in this hall is the painted ceiling. At one time most of the *mandapa* ceilings of Vijayanagar were painted and this is the best preserved one. Painted in the primary colours of red, green, blue and gold, the panels are narrative paintings showing Hindu myths and legends. The main one is on the marriage of Pampa and Virupaksha, episodes from the Ramayana and also other myths of Shiva, like of Tripurari, the warrior-god, who destroyed three demon worlds with one arrow. As with all living temples where repairs and additions go on continuously, it is hard to authenticate the date of this painting. During such renovations some panels may have been added, like one corner panel that shows Vidyaranya

An open pillared hall in a temple precinct is used for religious ceremonies, feeding of the poor and even to house pilgrims.

Devi Durga, a goddess in the aspect of a warrior, carrying many weapons including a sword.

being carried in a palanquin and the accompanying figures bearing guns were probably modelled on soldiers from the 18th century. The entrance has two giant doormen carved in granite; these *dvarapala*s have four arms and are 2.7 metres tall.

Worshippers enter the sanctum from a door on the left. The sanctum is quite small and the deity is a *Shivalingam* with a golden mask called a *Mukhalingam*. Domingo Paes claimed that he managed to get inside the temple and even entered the sanctum. His description matches with what we see today as he wrote, 'All the outer side of the gate of the temple (doorway of the main shrine) up to the roof is covered with copper and gilded, and on each side of the roof on the top are certain great animals that look like tigers, all gilt.' Of the lamp-stands he wrote, 'A pillar on which it is supported many little holes in which stand oil lamps, which burn so they tell me, every night, and they will be in number two thousand five hundred or three thousand.'

Coming out on the other side of the sanctum, there are the *amman* shrines of Pampa and Bhuvaneshwari. These are simpler structures. Bhuvaneshwari's temple has rather interesting columns in a dark green stone that are a pretty contrast to the surrounding granite. There are a number of smaller shrines around the courtyard including one dedicated to Vidyaranya and an ancient one with a rather worn image of Mahishasuramardini – showing a ten-armed Goddess Durga, rampant on a lion, slaying a demon. At this end of the court is a small gateway called the Kanakagiri *gopuram* that leads out of the temple complex towards the temple tank called the Manmatha Sarovar. This pool with steps painted in red and white stripes has many small shrines on its banks.

Hampi Bazaar...

A Hindu temple is not just a religious centre; it is also a commercial one, so shops rise along its main avenue to cater to worshippers. Indians often combine a holiday with a pilgrimage, so the temple bazaar would not only have shops selling the paraphernalia of worship – the flowers, fruits, incense, brass and copper bowls and the icons – but also shops selling textiles, jewellery, pottery and wood ware and have restaurants and hotels. The four most important temples

in Vijayanagar – Virupaksha, Vitthala, Achyut Raya's Tiruvengalanatha and Krishna – all had bazaar roads with colonnaded arcades attached to them and the chariot festival would wend its way along this road. Some of these bazaar streets like the one of the Krishna Temple have now been turned into paddy and sugarcane fields but the most famous of all, Hampi Bazaar still survives, even though it is in a very dilapidated state.

At the ends of the Hampi Bazaar are two low rocky hills – Hemkuta behind the Virupaksha Temple and Matanga. It is a generously laid out avenue – 10.6 metres wide and 732 metres in length – and all the foreign travellers write of the dazzling arcade of shops on both sides. On one end is the outer *gopuram* of the Virupaksha Temple and the road has rows of pillared alcoves on both sides that once held the shops. A few closer to the temple still have rather primitive stalls but further down the avenue the colonnade is deserted. At the other end is an open pavilion with a stone image of the Nandi Bull, still majestic in spite of being badly mutilated. Before it is a two-storey open pillared building with early Chalukyan style pillars which did not have the florid carvings of the Vijayanagar style. During the annual chariot festival these empty spaces fill up with pilgrims and Hampi Bazaar comes alive again.

Temples on Hemkuta Hill...

On the hill beside the Virupaksha Temple are a cluster of temples that look quite different from the rest of the nearby shrines. The temples are built along the sheer granite face of the hill and to reach them you have to take the lane beside the eastern *gopuram* of the Virupaksha that enters the Hampi village. The narrow path weaves up the hill and a simple gate leads up the slope to the temples that were built before the Vijayanagar period. There are no steps and one has to walk along the slope and this is a slightly difficult climb.

These are simple, rather austere buildings, built all in stone. Most of them have three sanctums with a small hall around them. The walls and ceilings are plain and the square pillars are carved with simple designs. There are no rampant *yali*s or prancing horses here but many simply carved deities and floral and geometric patterns. The granite towers are what make the shrines so different as they are all in stone and built in neat pyramids in symmetrical, stepped layers and without any brick or plaster. Being all in stone these temples have survived much better than the other temples in Hampi.

Some of the structures look much older than the rest with

Intricate ceiling details of the Vitthala maha mandapa.

Facing page: *The long arcade of the Hampi Bazaar that starts at the Matanga Hill and ends at the Virupaksha Temple.*

primitive carvings and floor plans that recall the Pallava School of the 8th century. One inscription says that Vira Kampiladeva installed three *Shivalingams* here in the early 14th century. Kampiladeva was the ruler of Kampili who employed Harihara and Bukka. So this dates it just before the establishment of the Vijayanagar Empire. Some of the temples are Shaiva shrines and others may have been dedicated to Ganesha as the pillar carvings often show the elephant-headed god in a dancing pose, as also goddesses and worshippers with elaborate plaited hair blowing conches.

In contrast to the silence in these shrines, nearby is a small, rather non-descriptive temple that still echoes to prayers, and white clad, bare-chested priests worship intoning Sanskrit *shloka*s. This temple is said to have been built by

Madhavacharya Vidyaranya, the spiritual guru of Harihara and Bukka. The sanctum has a *Mukhalingam* with a golden mask and a serpent hood curving over it called Ramalingeshwara. Vidyaranya is said to have built his ashram, his spiritual retreat here on the summit of the Hemkuta and it is easy to understand why he chose this spot. In spite of being within walking distance of the Hampi Bazaar, it is secluded and serenely peaceful. The river shines silver in the sun as it flows below and the sound of the temple bells flow out through the air from Virupaksha's shrine.

Giant Ganeshas...

On the opposite slope of the Hemkuta Hill, facing away from the Virupaksha Temple are two huge and oddly beguiling images of the elephant-headed Ganesha, the kindest and most generous god of the Hindu pantheon. In fact, these two open pavilions are the first Hampi monuments that you encounter going up the hill on the road from Hospet. The open *mandapa*s with slender, square carved pillars have a classic and very pleasing elegance and within it are two monolith images of Ganesha carved in the round from single boulders.

The Ganeshas, with typical Indian tongue-in-cheek humour, are named after two tiny Indian food grains. The first one, a massive 2.4 metres high, is affectionately referred to as *Sasivekalu* or the Mustard Seed Ganesha. The other even bigger at 4.5 metres, is happily titled *Kadalekalu* or Gram Lentil Ganesha. They act as a welcoming guard on the path that leads down from the summit of the hill to the Hampi Bazaar.

Facing page: *View on the slope of the Hemkuta Hill.*

Even in their mutilated form the two images of a god, who loves to eat and is happily fat have a special charm. *Sasivekalu* wears a snake as a belt around his generous belly and *Kadalekalu*'s trunk is nuzzling into a bowl of sweet *modak*s as his pet rat sits patiently at his feet. Pause here by the pavilions for a while and look around you at an unparalleled panorama of the monuments of Hampi. For most visitors this is their first view of the remains of Vijayanagar and this heart-stopping cityscape remains with them for ever.

Achyut Raya's Temple...

Hampi Bazaar ends at the Matanga Hill and at the other side of this teetering pile of boulders is a walled temple complex with the collapsed remains of a bazaar street that is popularly called Achyut Raya's Temple after the king who built it. The inscriptions in the temple (also called Tiruvengalanatha Temple) tell us that it was dedicated to Lord Tiruvengalanatha, an aspect of Lord Vishnu.

For the energetic, willing to clamber up the rocky incline of the Matanga Hill, the bird's eye view of the temple complex from the top is a perfect way to understand the traditional layout of Hindu temples in Hampi. The central sanctum of the *garbha griha* and *amman* shrine to the Goddess Lakshmi, surrounded by a colonnaded wall, the two *prakara* courtyards, the three *gopuram* gateways and the *mandapa*, the open pillared hall, they are all there, placed with precision. The mellow red-gold walls stand framed by hills, palm and banana groves and the blue sky, creating a living, landscape painting.

Facing page: *The giant Ganesha, called* Sasivekalu, *who welcomes visitors to Hampi with a benign smile.*

Another easier path is to take a left turn at the fork of the Hampi Bazaar and you'll find yourself on a hill path weaving by the banks of the Tungabhadra. Walk on, past the river ghat, the Kodandarama Temple and then turn right and you'll find yourself at the end of the bazaar street of Achyut Raya's temple. Inscriptions within the precinct say that it was built in AD 1534 by Hiriya Tirumalaraja, the brother-in-law of King Achyut Raya who succeeded Krishnadeva to the throne.

As this temple is hidden behind a hill and stands away from the bustle of Hampi Bazaar, it is often quiet and deserted. Pause here to sit in the open porch and listen to the ancient ghosts, feel the unique ambience and wander about to study the sculptures. You'll discover there is a very different light that flows through the

A view of the Tiruvengalanatha Temple built by King Achyut Raya from the top of Matanga Hill.

granite hallways and angles away from the silent courtyards. The sun filters past the pillars, curves down from the eaves in a gentle, red-gold shadowy gleam; playfully picking out the edge of a dancing *yakshi*, gleaming on a rearing horse. The light is gentle and soothing inside, bright and harsh as you step out.

Then as you sit and listen, you'll become conscious of the silence, nearly palpable like a buzz, where every flutter of a pigeon's wings or the wind flowing through palm fronds is clearly heard. The silence is oddly alive as the peace envelops you completely and you'll discover another magic of Hampi – its ability to bring a sense of generous serenity. However, this is a temple that has not been alive in centuries, there is no deity to worship in the dark and deserted *garbha griha* but the hymns and mantras still seem to flow through the air.

The main *gopuram* gateway's tower has collapsed into a confusion of bricks. It faces the east and leads out to the rows of teetering pillars and lintels of the Soolai Bazaar. Once this temple was at the heart of the locality of Achyutapura and the bazaar led down to the river. Legends say that once the most beautiful courtesans of Vijayanagar had their mansions around the Soolai and the bazaar saw the chariots and palanquins of princes and noblemen. Here the dancing girls sat, dressed to seduce, their diamonds winking in the sun; their gold and silks shimmering in the lamp light. There are the remains of a water pool at the end of the street with a tiny pavilion in the middle, called the Dancing Girl's Bath. Now weeds and brambles grow among the collapsed columns and the road is rutted by bullock cart tracks and you walk along the silent street by the slipping shade of the tilting, dilapidated arcade.

Kodandarama Temple...

Coming out of the Virupaksha Temple, walk down Hampi Bazaar and before you reach the Nandi Bull, take a left towards the hilly path that wend its way by the river to the Kodandarama Temple. Along this path is the Chakratirtha, the most sacred bathing ghat of Pampakshetra. Here the Tungabhadra curves north to flow through a boulder-strewn gorge. Below the cliff the river swirls around boulders and the pilgrims bathe in the clear water, drying brightly coloured saris on the sandy banks and sitting in huddles for impromptu picnics. Beyond are the pylons of an ancient bridge, the stark abandoned pillars standing out of the water like bare tree trunks after a storm, mysterious spikes spanning the turbulent waters.

The bathing ghat has a spreading peepal tree on top with a *deepa sthambha*, a lamp-stand, and many naga stones that are granite slabs carved with the image of snakes that worshippers place near temples

Left: *The Kodandarama Temple is one of the living shrines at Hampi and stands by the banks of the Tungabhadra.*

Middle: *A wall carving showing Sita from the Ramayana.*

Right: *Hampi is believed to be ancient Kishkindha of the Ramayana, so Hanuman is one of the most popular images.*

after their prayers are answered. Behind the steps of the ghat stands the Kodandarama Temple; it is an active temple in the circuit of pilgrims who head here after their puja to Lord Virupaksha. The sanctum has the huge, bas-relief images of Lord Ram, Sita, Lakshman and Hanuman. The images are 4.5 metres high and carved out of a natural boulder. Legends connected to the Ramayana say that Sugriva was crowned here as the king of Kishkindha after Ram had killed his rival Valli. Beyond the temple there is a lovely image of Vishnu as *anantashayana* carved on a rock. It shows the reclining god with Lord Brahma sitting on a lotus that is growing out of his navel.

Krishna Temple...

Krishnadeva Raya's temple to Lord Krishna stands by the road that starts at Hampi Bazaar and goes to the Royal Enclosure around Kamalapura village. This temple like the Achyut Raya shrine was at the centre of a city quarter called Krishnapura. Also like all the other important temples, it has a colonnaded bazaar street stretching away from its main *gopuram*. However, this temple has no deity and it sees only sightseers not worshippers. The road cuts through the bazaar avenue and the arcades now stand rather incongruously among paddy fields and banana groves.

The Krishnaswami Temple was built by Krishnadeva Raya in AD 1513 after his victory over the Gajapati of Orissa. He had recaptured the fortress of Udayagiri and brought back a granite icon of Balagopal, the infant Lord Krishna, which was enshrined in the sanctum. Today the image can be seen at the Chennai Museum. There are three *gopuram*s and the largest must have been a majestic

one, the granite base is wide and generously carved but the brick and plaster pyramidal top is badly dilapidated. The carvings have some sublime motifs – sinuous maidens leaning against curving vines, snakes, animals and deities. Look up at the ruined stucco work on top and you'll see fragments of battle scenes, so probably the story of the king's victory at Udayagiri was etched here.

In the courtyard there is an inscribed slab that recounts Krishnadeva's military triumphs. The inner precinct has many halls and small shrines, including an unusual one to the warrior god, Lord

The ruined gopuram *that leads into the Krishna Temple.*

Facing page: *Many villages surround the ruins of Vijayanagar. Here a hill top view of rural Hampi.*

Subramanya, riding on his peacock. The *mandapa* halls have all the sculptural elements of the period – the various kinds of composite pillars, the elaborately carved ceilings and outer walls. Look for the pillar that depicts Vishnu's avatars, the ten incarnations of Vishnu worked out in precise bas-relief.

Narasimha Statue...

This giant monolith granite image of Narasimha, the man-lion incarnation of Vishnu is one of the most popular visual symbols of Vijayanagar and Hampi. As the road meanders past sugarcane fields, a narrow path on the right goes past an open pavilion and a temple with a giant *Shivalingam,* half-submerged in water. Then to the left, in the middle of a walled enclosure, the Narasimha statue looms over the tall sugarcane, impressively huge and oddly beguiling for all its terrible aspect. No photograph can capture the sheer, gigantic majesty of this image. There he sits in a yogic posture, 6.7 metres tall, cross-legged with that threatening fanged grin and once the body of the demon Hiranyakasipu must have lain prostrate across the immense lap. A seven-headed Naga snake spreads its hood on top and the image is framed by a *makara torana* arch.

As the inscription on a granite slab nearby states, it was commissioned by Krishnadeva in AD 1528 and carved out of a single boulder by a Brahmin named Krishnabhatta. Ultimately the image would probably have been enclosed in a pavilion like the two Ganeshas but the *mandapa* was never built. Even though very badly mutilated, it is still a magnificent and powerful image of the man-lion, with fierce fangs and protuberant eyes. It has four arms and

Facing page: *The magnificent image of Lord Narasimha, an avatar of Lord Vishnu that has become a symbol of Vijayanagar.*

once Goddess Lakshmi, the Goddess of Wealth rested on his left thigh but now only a fragment of her arm encircling his waist survives, the rest lies in pieces below.

It was dusk when I first saw the Narasimha. As I stood mesmerised, the setting sun dipped down behind the image and a streak of sunlight flashed past the shadowy head. I was shaken by its monstrous majesty, a brute, domineering power and then I remembered it was fashioned by a man, with just a hammer and chisel.

Other Temples...

There are numerous other temples that are worth visiting if you have the time. Many are important to pilgrims because of their association with religious myths and legends. However these are not the best examples of temple architecture.

The Pattabhirama Temple stands on the outskirts of Kamalapura, near Hampi's Archaeological Museum. It was built by Varadevi, one of the queens of Achyut Raya. It has a complex as large as the Vitthala Temple but with an austere plan of simple pillared *mandapa*s.

The Ganagitti Jain Temple means the 'oil woman's temple', though no one has an explanation for the odd name. It stands along the same road

Vitthala Temple with its tiered brick gopuram *and high stone plinth.*

The Ganagitti Jain Temple is also called 'the oil-woman's temple'.

and is a simple, rather plain building. The inscription on the lamp-stand says it was built in by Irugappa, a general of Bukka II and was dedicated to the Jain saint Kunthu Jinanatha.

The Malayavanta Raghunatha Temple is associated with the legend of Ram and stands atop the Malayavanta Hill. The hill is on the road going towards Kampili village on way to the Telarigattu Ghat. Its sanctum is attached to a large boulder on which the images of Ram, Sita, Lakshman and Hanuman are carved. At the back a cleft in the rock is said to have been caused by Ram's arrow and it has been surrounded with carved rows of *Shivalingam*s and Nandi bulls.

HINDU ARCHITECTURAL TERMS

amman shrine – temple to the mother-goddess
antarala – ante chamber before the sanctum
ardha mandapa – an annex before the sanctum
bhoga mandapa – refectory hall
deepa sthambha – stand for holding lamps
garbha griha – sanctum sanctorum
gopuram – monumental temple gateway
kalyana mandapa – hall of marriage
maha mandapa – the main audience hall
mandala – symbol of the cosmos
mandapa – open pillared hall
natya mandapa – dance hall
pradakshina patha – ambulatory passage
prakara – open courtyard enclosed by a wall
ranga mandapa – painted hall or theatre
ratha – temple chariot
shikhara – temple spire
vimana – the sanctum and the spire
yali – mythical lion-like beast

View of an ancient landscape that is redolent with myths and legends that hark back to the epic, the Ramayana.

Chapter Seven

A QUIET PAUSE AT VITTHALA

Experience the ambience at a unique temple

The Vitthala Temple portrays the high watermark of perfection of the Vijayanagar style, and one may well say that there is no other building which could stand comparison with it in florid magnificence.

– D Devakunjari

7

The generous spirit of Krishnadeva Raya still permeates the air at the Vitthala Temple, the finest creation of his reign and by far the grandest shrine in Hampi. The temple stands near the river, along a dusty path leading away from the Hampi Bazaar. As one enters under the broken southern *gopuram,* there is an expansive courtyard with the main temple set in the middle. On the right stands the temple to the goddess and at the other corners of the temple precinct there are other open pillared pavilions of different sizes. The original entrance must have been through another *gopuram* facing east because the remains of a bazaar street stretch away beyond it. Between this *gopuram* and the front porch of the main audience hall, stands a stone replica of a temple chariot that is as much a visual symbol of Vijayanagar as the statue of Narasimha.

Lord Vitthala is an aspect of Vishnu and the oldest shrine to this deity is in Pandharpur, Maharashtra. Records show that there was a temple here even during the reign of Deva Raya II (AD 1424-46) and other kings added to it. The *maha mandapa* was probably built by Krishnadeva, who also built a 100-pillared hall and two of his queens added the *gopurams*. Today the sanctum stands empty and

Pillars carved with the mythical half-lion–half-horse creature called yali.

Facing page: *The exquisite stone chariot at the Vitthala Temple which once had a brick superstructure.*

The maha mandapa *and the* kalyana mandapa *of the Vitthala Temple that housed the image of the goddess consort of the deity.*

Pages 202–03: *A view of the ruined* gopuram *and the courtyard of the Vitthala Temple.*

the walls and ceilings still bear signs of a fire. One tradition says that the temple was never finished nor consecrated and the story goes that Vitthala came here from Pandharpur and found the temple much too elaborate and went back to his simple shrine. However, inscriptions have been found dating from AD 1513 to 1564 and literary and epigraphic evidence shows that there was worship here till the Battle of Talikota in AD 1565. As D Devakunjari writes, 'it portrays the high watermark of perfection of the Vijayanagar style, and one may well say that there is no other building which could stand comparison with it in florid magnificence.'

This temple is like a copybook of the perfect temple in the Dravidian School of sacred architecture. It has all the architectural elements of a shrine—the *garbha griha* (sanctum), the *pradakshina patha* (ambulatory passage), the *antarala* (vestibule) that connects the sanctum to the *maha mandapa* (main audience hall); then out in the *prakara* (courtyard)—the temple to the *amman* shrine (celestial consort) and *mandapa*s (smaller pavilions) nearby. The three *gopuram*s lead into the enclosure and a pillared colonnade runs along the interior of the wall. What is special about Vitthala is that everything is more rich and elaborate, the carvings have a vibrant flair and the design of the halls exhibit a generous elegance of space. There is a joyous exuberance to the sculpture as if the artists were working in wood or clay and not intractable stone.

The finest monument here is the sumptuous *maha mandapa*. It stands on a broad carved plinth, and before you enter the hall, walk outside enjoying the carvings along its length. There are the marching men, dancing women and animals but also charming

Delicate columns surround the elegantly carved pillars of the Vitthala Temple.

rows of happy geese. The balustrades of the steps going up to the porches are in the shape of elephants and sinuous snakes. Inside, the main attraction of the *mandapa* are the pillars carved in endless variety. Here the proud, triumphant spirit of Vijayanagar is captured perfectly in stone.

One can spend a whole morning just wandering along its bays of fifty-six pillars marvelling at the limitless imaginative verve of the carvings. The sun pours in past these pillars and the prancing horses, the mythical *yali*s and caparisoned elephants seem to come alive in the shifting red-gold light. The outer rows have the lion-like *yali*s and hippogryphs, rearing up arrogantly, baring their teeth in a threatening grin and often with a rider on their backs. If you study the riders carefully you'll notice that some of them have beards like Muslim fighters. There are also some figures carved in the round like the 2.7 metre tall, broken figure of a *dvarapala*, a doorman, who still stands patiently at the sanctum door.

The pillars along the porch facing the stone chariot are different, with a broad central beam surrounded by a circle of delicate, thin columns that according to Percy Brown form, 'a girdle of detached shafts of most graceful and elegant proportions'. The local guides claim that these are musical pillars that play all the notes of the musical scale. Do discourage them from energetically tapping at the pillars to prove their point as this will further damage the fragile columns. The claim is clearly the inspired invention of some guide in the past because it takes a lot of gullible imagination to believe that there is anything remotely musical about their desperate tapping.

Strolling around looking at the carvings you realise that there is no apparent symmetry in the pillars but surprisingly it all blends in a perfect whole. There are bas-reliefs of the ten incarnations of Vishnu and the crouching Narasimha appears often, also other gods and goddesses especially Ganesha, Krishna, Lakshmi and Saraswati, as well as Ram, Sita and Hanuman in his characteristic profile with the curving tail. Men worshipping, women dancing with their skirts flaring, elephants, horses, Nandi bulls, snakes, crocodiles, trees and flowers—all crowd on the walls. Also there appears at places an amusing jester-like figure in a belled cap, his knees bent comically, holding a rattle in each hand.

If you study the pillars carefully you'll realise that they show various levels of skills. Some are quite simple with straight geometrical sides and floral patterns while others teem with intricately chiselled images. It was as if each sculptor was handed a block of stone and allowed complete freedom and then the carved pillars were put up as they were completed. The un-matching style makes every pillar a revelation and you discover newer motifs at every step. Unlike the disciplined symmetry of Christian and Islamic design, it is uniquely Hindu because in Hinduism worship is personal and idiosyncratic and not regimented. Hindu deities are more loved than feared and creative freedom comes naturally, in fact, rigid symmetry is not in the Indian nature. Peering down to study a benign goddess or a delicately carved lotus bud I thought of the long forgotten sculptors who laboured over these stones, who at times must have carved the face of a beloved woman on a goddess or their own child on Krishna holding a ball of butter. This unpredictable creativity has a very special enchantment.

A bird's eye view of the temple complex of the shrine of Vitthala.

Following page: *The King's Balance where a king was weighed against gold, silver or grains that were then given in charity.*

Pause at the *maha mandapa,* sit leaning against a pillar and let the ambience seep into you. Imagine what this majestic hall must have been like when Krishnadeva came here for worship during the festivals. There would be carpets on the floor, tall lamp-stands glowing with lights and lamps hanging from the brackets on top of the pillars, incense smoking up from bowls. As the priest raised the many-flamed *arati* lamp to illumine the face of the god, the *devadasi*s would begin to dance with a jangle of anklets. The air would reverberate to the chanting of mantras and the blowing of conches as the flaring camphor lit up the sanctum. The dancers would flit past the pillars shimmering in silks, with their diamond jewellery flashing in the light. They would worship their Lord Vitthala through their dance with the drums, flutes and *manjira* keeping beat to their flying hands and feet. And beyond, in the dim, lamp-lit sanctum stands – the remote, Godhead's jewelled eyes watching over them all – the Supreme Vitthala.

The stone *ratha*, the chariot car, sits facing the eastern *gopuram*. There are four wheels that could be turned and the small shrine within the pillared top has the image of the sacred bird of Vishnu, Garuda. Originally, it must have been topped by a brick and plaster tower but it has vanished. Oddly, two elephants stand where the horses of the chariot should have been placed.

Among the other *mandapa*s in the courtyard the most decorative is the *kalyana mandapa*. It is ornate and feminine as a celestial marriage pavilion should be. The delicately carved ceiling has inverted lotuses and still carries patches of parrot green paint from the time when the whole pavilion would have been white-washed and brightly coloured. Inside there is a central platform where the icons would have been placed during the wedding

ceremony and it is surrounded by piers of pillars. The other halls include a hundred-pillared *mandapa* built by Krishnadeva and two smaller pavilions at the corners of the courtyard.

The courtyard of the Vitthala Temple has a number of open pillared halls where pilgrims take rest.

Coming out of Vitthala if you take the footpath that leads to the Tungabhadra, the sides are strewn with small, nameless shrines and pavilions, often with pillars but no roofs. The path goes past a double-storeyed gateway and then under a stone arch called the King's Balance where tradition says the *Tulapurusha-dana* ritual was held. At this ceremony on the king's birthday he was weighed against gold, jewels and grain and it was distributed among the people.

Chapter Eight

AN IMPERIAL CITADEL

The majestic architecture of the Royal Enclosure

There can be little doubt that this platform represents the remains of the magnificent pavilion in which was placed the wonderful royal throne of gold and gems used by the sovereign during the Mahanavami or great nine day's festival.

– A H Longhurst

8

If you were travelling to Vijayanagar by boat during its heyday you would have alighted at the Telarigattu Ghat on the Tungabhadra. The stone steps of the main landing stage stood across the river from the Anegondi Fort of Kampiladeva. One can still see the hoary walls of the ancient fortress rising broodingly across the water and can take one of the round boats to go across the river. From this ghat, a broad thoroughfare lined with shops led to the royal enclave, the walled innermost citadel where the king and the royal family lived.

This road, popularly called Paan Supari Rasta, rivalled the Hampi Bazaar in its magnificence and as it was not connected to a temple, it was a much more sophisticated and cosmopolitan avenue. It glittered with shops selling silks and muslins as ethereal as spider's web, rare gems and jewellery crafted in gold and silver, metal and wood ware, pottery, flowers, paan and perfumes. This was where the nobility stepped out of palanquins for some languid shopping and visits to the taverns and gambling dens and courtesans at the doors of their mansions would invite them in with a flirtatious swirl of their saris.

Carvings of a warrior battling a bear.

Facing page: *The tiered gateway leading to the Telarigattu Ghat. A road that bustled with shops linked this ghat with the royal enclave.*

All that vivid, iridescent life is long gone. Today Telarigattu is a small flight of steps leading up from the river to a rather dilapidated gateway and beyond it is just a narrow road winding its lonely way among an expanse of boulder-strewn land with patches of fortification walls and an occasional watchtower or lookout pavilion on a distant ridge. The imperial city faced the greatest destruction after the defeat at the Battle of Talikota in AD 1565 and most of the structures vanished. Unlike the temples that were built all in stone, the palaces had stone plinths over which the building was erected in wood, bricks and plaster. So when the Muslim invaders ruthlessly set fire to them they were totally obliterated and all that remains today are the empty granite basements that can only give an idea of the gorgeous palaces that once stood on them.

Left: *The basement of a palace in the* zenana *enclosure.*

Right: *The* zenana *area or the women's quarters was the personal space of the royal family, was surrounded by high walls pierced by watchtowers.*

Pages 216–17: *The Lotus Mahal is one of the few structures in the Royal Enclosure that have survived intact.*

So what remains in the imperial zone are the many-tiered and carved platforms over which the palaces had been built that dazzled the foreign visitors, the collapsing citadel walls with gateways, watchtowers, the bathing pools, the remains of the stone aqueducts and a few temples. The king's apartments, the audience halls, the harem, the homes of the nobility, the royal offices, the stores, soldier's quarters and stables have all vanished. Most of the time archaeologists and historians are merely guessing at the purpose of a structure, looking for clues in inscriptions and trying to match it against the accounts of a foreign traveller. No one can be certain of what the palaces looked like and what happened in them.

The octagonal Bath once had a fountain splashing water in the middle and may have been used by the royal men.

The great imperial metropolis that was compared to Rome by Domingo Paes is irrevocably lost and a visitor has to imagine its majesty and power, standing in the middle of the destruction wrecked by a senseless, violent religious malice that could not bear to let such beauty exist. Royal Vijayanagar paid the ultimate price for its extravagant, generous and tolerant spirit; it ceased to exist.

Fortifications...

The Persian ambassador, Abdur Razzaq arriving in Vijayanagar during the reign of Deva Raya II in AD 1443 describes the city as being surrounded by seven concentric layers of walls.

It is built in such a manner that seven citadels and the same number of walls enclose each other... The fortress is in the form of a circle, situated on the summit of a hill, and is made of stone and mortar, with strong gates where guards are always posted, who are very diligent in the collection of taxes. The seventh fortress is placed in the centre of the others, and within that is situated the palace of the king.

According to these chronicles, the Royal Enclosure was an oval-shaped walled space that held the royal palaces, audience chambers, parade grounds, the harem, temples, offices, mint, stores, stables, guard's quarters and all the other buildings of a city's centre.

Vijayanagar was the largest city in India at that time, much more magnificent and prosperous than other capitals like the Sultanate Delhi or the Bahmani Gulbarga. The walls surrounded an area of twenty-six square kilometres with the northern outpost at Anegondi, the eastern at Kampili and the southern wall running down to Hospet. The walls were built with large blocks of dressed granite that were used without any form of cementing, just cut to fit together, with earth poured in between as filling. In fact, the walls were not really as strong as they looked and it is remarkable how much has still survived. An aerial survey shows the extent of the fortification with remnants of all the seven encircling walls being visible. The remains of the moat that ran along some parts of the walls can also be seen and it clearly shows Telarigattu Ghat as being the main entrance to the imperial city.

The walls enclosed small towns and villages that fell within the greater metropolitan area of Vijayanagar. These included towns like Hospet, Kampili and Anegondi and villages like Hampi,

Kamalapuram, Malpannagudi, Kadirampuram and Anantashayanagudi, and all of them still exist. Abdur Razzaq writes that 'between the first, second and third walls there are cultivated fields, gardens and houses. From the third to the seventh – fortress, shops and bazaars are closely crowded together.' Even today farmers work in their paddy and sugarcane fields with ancient pavilions in the middle and use stone from the walls to prop up the roof of their red-tiled homes and women dry their brightly coloured saris on patches of collapsed pillars; as they all live serenely among the ruins with that typically Indian acceptance of the rise and fall of history.

The many gates that pierced the walls were often visually pleasing creations and as D Devakunjari writes, they illustrate 'the expert skills with which the Hindu artisans converted utilitarian works into things of beauty'. Often the gates had barbicans with a curved entrance to stop the enemy cavalry from charging in and the main roads were paved in stone. The gates are at times double-storeyed with arched entrances, with scrolls carved out in stucco and domed roofs and some have a distinctly Islamic design. The walls are carved in bas-relief showing many scenes of everyday life like a king in the typical tall headdress worshipping a *Shivalingam*

or images from mythology and epics. The most eye-catching is the Bhima Gate with ornamental brackets on top of the pillars and arches leading into the guard's rooms. On one large slab there is a carved image of Bhima, one of the heroes of the epic, the Mahabharata. In one panel he is shown killing the villain Kichaka who had tried to assault Bhima's wife Draupadi and she stands nearby watching.

Hazara Rama Temple...

When you turn into the innermost citadel area from the main road, the path divides into two—the left leads to the *zenana* and the right to the Royal Enclosure. The Hazara Rama Temple is the first monument on the right. This is the most ornate and well-preserved

Lord Ram, Sita and Lakshman carved on the outer wall of the Hazara Rama Temple.

Previous page: *A row of Islamic arches provide an airy space inside one of the Guard's Quarters of the Royal Enclosure.*

temple in the royal zone and as the name suggests it is dedicated to Ram, the eighth incarnation of Lord Vishnu, but as the sanctum is empty it cannot be confirmed. The name 'Hazara Rama' sounds like a temple for a thousand Rams but Telugu historians point out that the Telugu word *hajaramu* means an entrance hall to a palace and the temple does stand at the entrance to the quadrangle that has the ruins of the main palaces.

The Hampi landscape is redolent with the episodes from the Ramayana and it is probably not a coincidence that the Matanga and Malayavanta hills that are connected to the epic can be viewed from this temple. It is much smaller than other important shrines like Virupaksha, Vitthala or Achyut Raya's temples and was probably the private chapel of the royal family. There is a Sanskrit inscription that begs for the blessings of Goddess Pampa for Deva Raya I and also there is no *gopuram* over the stone gateway, so probably the temple was built during his reign. The *kalyana mandapa* was added during the reign of Krishnadeva Raya. There is only one courtyard with the main temple, an *amman* shrine, a *kalyana mandapa* and a few smaller shrines.

What makes this temple a very special experience is the carvings on the outer walls that tell the story of the Ramayana in a unique graphic form. There are 108 scenes from the Ramayana carved in panels divided by elegant pilasters with lotus brackets that begin with Valmiki narrating the story and King Dasaratha's fire sacrifice praying for a son. Chiselled with amazing delicacy these exquisite bas-relief carvings are like a picture gallery of the epic. One panel shows Sita's *swayamvar* with men struggling to carry the giant bow of Shiva and another where Ravana is changing from a sadhu into a ten-headed demon. Among the others is Ram sitting under a

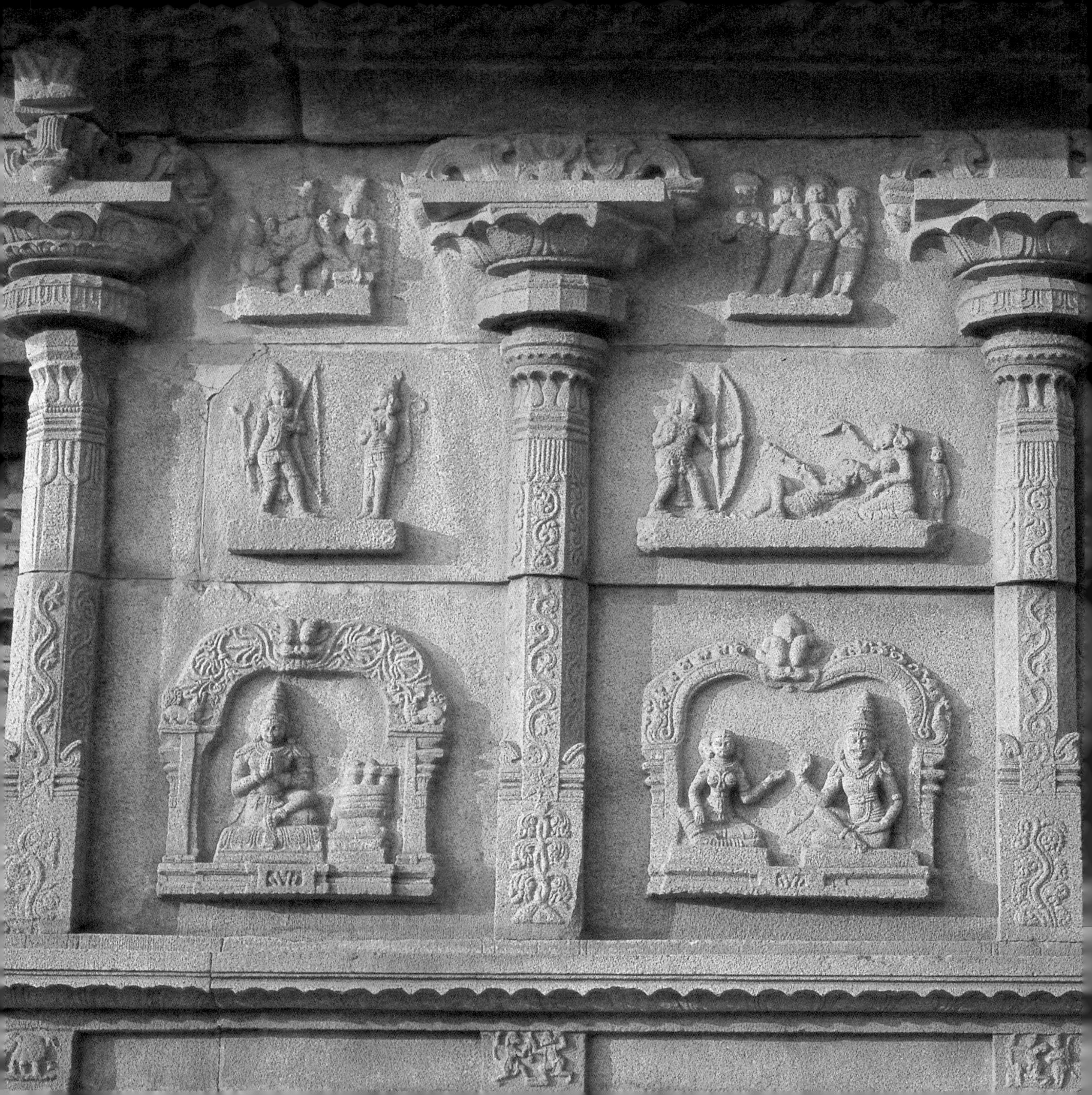

108 scenes from the Ramayana are depicted on the outer walls of the Hazara Rama Temple.

tree with Lakshman standing beside him, as he gives his ring to Hanuman; another of Sita giving her hair ornament to Hanuman and the Monkey God's leap over the sea.

The main shrine has pyramidal domes on the roof and inside there are four polished black stone pillars with carvings of Ganesha, Durga and Hanuman. The forms of the ten avatars of Vishnu can be seen everywhere, the young Krishna holding a ball of butter is among the most charming and they can be seen even on the outside of the precinct walls. There is also a small shrine dedicated to Narasimha, the lion-headed incarnation of Vishnu. The *amman* shrine has two storeys with a wagon-shaped roof and must have housed an image of Goddess Lakshmi as she is the consort of Vishnu. Krishnadeva was a Vaishnava and must have worshipped here and the *kalyana mandapa* built by him is the most ornate structure in this temple courtyard. There is a narrow path that connects the temple to the palace area and was probably used by the king to visit the temple.

Mahanavami Dibba and Other Platforms...

Beyond the Hazara Rama Temple one enters the heart of Vijayanagar, the imperial citadel. It is an expansive open space and as far as the eye can see there are the remnants of walls and palaces. What catches the visitor's attention immediately are a number of giant tiered granite platforms that appear to be intriguing because at first sight one cannot understand what they could possibly have been for. These were once the basements of luxurious palaces that were erected on top in brick, wood and plaster and decorated with precious metal and gems.

One can only guess at what the palaces looked like and what they were used for – the royal apartments, the audience halls, the harem or the offices of the bureaucracy. All that remains on the floor of the top tiers are rows of sockets made for the wooden pillars and the carvings on the sides that can be matched against the chronicle of the travellers. Percy Brown captures perfectly the majestic mystery of these platforms as he writes,

> *Even in their dismantled condition these elevated and orderly piles of masonry with their finely moulded revetments retain some of the glamour and romance of that brilliant period when Vijayanagar, the 'City of Victory' was one of the most famous capitals of the East.*

The Mahanavami Dibba is the largest platform and the site of the famous Mahanavami festival every year.

One finds a description of the interiors of the palaces in the writings of Domingo Paes. He writes of one: 'It has a four-sided porch made of cane-work over which is a work of rubies and diamonds and all other kinds of precious stones, and pearls and above the porch are two pendants of gold.' Then he describes an extraordinary room: 'there is a room with pillars of carved stone; this room is all of ivory, as well as the chamber as the walls, from top to bottom... at the top had roses and flowers of lotuses all of ivory.' Then he admires Krishnadeva's throne observing:

> *It is four sided and flat, with a round top, and a hollow in the middle for the seat... It is covered with silk cloth and has lions all of gold, and in the spaces between the cloths with many rubies and seed pearls underneath; and round the sides it is full of golden images of personages.*

The carvings of these dancing women with their flaring saris can be seen in every panel showing a procession.

Reading the accounts of Paes and Fernao Nuniz as they describe the Mahanavami festival you realise that the gorgeous parade must have taken place in this quadrangle before the platform called the Mahanavami Dibba. This nine-day festival, also called Navaratri and Dussara is still celebrated in India in autumn. It was much more than a religious occasion at Vijayanagar; it was a triumphant celebration of royal power. The nobility arrived to pay their annual tribute to the king; the army marched and successful generals were awarded; bejewelled temples dancers and musicians performed; there were wrestling matches and animal sacrifices. The most vivid and detailed description is given by Paes about the Mahanavami celebrations after Krishnadeva's defeat of the Gajapati of Orissa.

Paes called the palace the 'House of Victory' and writes that it was built by Krishnadeva; other travellers refer to it as the Throne Platform and it is the largest plinth here. Dominating the area, it is built in three diminishing tiers with the base being forty metres square and the top floor twenty-four metres square and half-way up there is a terraced walkway. Every inch of the granite sides is covered in rows of running friezes of the processions that are crudely carved but with a joyous animation that is irresistible. One can spend a whole day just strolling around the platform making serendipitous discoveries. At times there are surprising humorous visuals among the more common dancing women, sacred geese, marching cavalry and archers. There are men in pointed caps bowing before the king that could be a Chinese embassy; Arab horse dealers with beards and caps; dancing jesters holding tambourines; a row of smiling camels in between the horses and elephants and exotic mythical animals. The western side was later covered in dark green chlorite and here the carving is even better. The platform is twelve metres high and has elephant balustrades along the steep stairs.

Among the dancers, marching men and prancing horses there are also camels and foreign visitors wearing strange caps.

The Mahanavami Dibba, once the scene of magnificent celebrations during the Mahanavami fesitival.

For an experience you will never forget, stand at the top of the Mahanavami Dibba as dusk slowly falls over Hampi. You will first see an incomparable panorama of Hampi and then watch the sun turn the sky orange as it sets over the shadowy ruins. As you wander around the top you'll notice a small chamber projecting from the platform connected by a flight of stairs. Historians speculate that the famous gold throne of the Vijayanagar kings may have been kept here. When you climb down walk around till you find another surprising creation – a giant door made of stone lying in pieces on the ground. The door is a perfect replica of a wooden one including bolt sockets and one wonders where it was used. Also nearby there is a giant trough 12.5 metres long, cut out of a single block of granite that may have been used to store water for horses.

A smaller platform located south-west of the Dibba (27mx18mx1.5m) is believed to be the plinth of the residence of the monarch. A broken elephant balustrade in green chlorite leads to the top and the sides have friezes like the ones at the Dibba. Near the palace base, an underground chamber made entirely of green chlorite has been discovered and it may have been the shrine where the king prayed during the ceremonies as described by Paes. He wrote, 'Then the king goes again to where the idol is, and as soon as he is inside they lift the purdahs of a tent and the king seats himself there.' Nearby a *yali* balustrade and a mutilated image of Lord Venugopal have been discovered and may have belonged to this mysterious chamber.

The Mahanavami parade must have been held in the open spaces before these palaces. There is also a third basement that matches with the chronicles of Abdur Razzaq and is called the King's Audience Hall. He had described a pillared building and here we can see the sockets for sixty pillars. Razzaq wrote, 'On the right hand of the palace there is the *diwan-khana* which is extremely large and presents the appearance of a *chihal-sutun* or forty pillared hall.' It is a tiered platform like the others but comparing the carvings they feel this was probably the earliest palace in the enclosure. Historians speculate that may be the women of the royal harem sat here to watch the Mahanavami celebrations.

Nearby there is an interesting square, bathing pool in a dark stone with a simple, rather Spartan design all in straight lines. The green chlorite Pushkarini Pool is connected to the snaking line of the aqueduct and it has square symmetrical steps that lead down to

Recent excavations have revealed a pool made with green chlorite in a complex geometric design.

the water. The precisely cut square steps in neat pyramids create a complex visual pattern in light and shade. Intriguingly, the steps have numbers carved on them; perhaps the pool was built somewhere else and reassembled here.

The Danaik Enclosure and the Mint...

There are some open spaces with the remains of palaces revealed by recent excavations that have been assigned names that are once again pure conjecture. The word 'Danaik' is a form of Dandanayaka meaning commander-in chief; though Abdur Razzaq describes a eunuch with the title of Danaik who sat in the administrative hall and was clearly an important personage as he had a man holding an umbrella over his head. This large area, now called the Danaik

Hampi continues to reveal new archaeological finds. Here the excavation site at the Danaik Enclosure.

Enclosure is again a walled area with the remains of buildings with pillar sockets and pillar bases. Another large walled courtyard west of the main palaces is called the Mint. More bases and bits of walls of buildings have been revealed here but nothing indicates that the royal mint operated from this area.

The *Zenana*...

Walk to the other end of the citadel to reach the walled area that is called the *zenana* or women's quarters. The name is a Muslim one just as one building inside is called a mahal. The surrounding wall is much higher than in any other part of the citadel and acts like a protective curtain and it was topped by iron spikes. There are three watchtowers at corners of the enclosure supporting the theory that it was the residence of the royal women and it also

A guard's lookout or may be a place from where the harem women could view the outside world.

The foliated arches that give a light, welcoming character to the Lotus Mahal.

has just one rather narrow entrance. Most historians including Longhurst and Devakunjari call this the *zenana* because of the high screen-like wall and the feminine buildings within but George Michell feels this may have been the personal living area of the king as the parade ground and Elephant Stables are nearby.

Inside the quadrangle one is once again confronted by the plinths of two vanished palaces and a dried-up bathing tank. Only two structures are still standing, one a pretty, arched building called the Lotus Mahal and another low, windowless rather gloomy looking structure designated as the Women's Guard's Quarters. There is also a small pavilion standing in the empty bathing pool.

The enchantingly feminine Lotus Mahal gives an idea of what the palaces may have looked like, even though this is a very small building. It is also called Chitragni Mahal and it is a miracle that it somehow survived the manic destruction by the invaders. The double-storeyed pillared pavilion has delicately curving floriated arches and once there must have been stucco and plaster ornamentation on the walls and pillars as one can see bits at some of the corners. The interior is simply ornamented but elegantly balanced, the vaulted ceiling rises to pendant lotus buds in the centre. The upper floor opens out into latticed balconies with tiny windows which once again indicate that women may have led secluded lives here. The central dome has an inverted lotus dome and the roof has nine pyramidal towers called *stupis*.

There is a Sultanate touch to be seen in the vaulted ceilings and the curvaceous arches. A H Longhurst categorises the Lotus Mahal as an Indo-Saracenic building, stating that, 'while the pillars and arches are Muhammadan in character, the base, roof, cornice and stucco ornaments are Hindu in design.' George Michell writes, 'These mixed origins make for a delightful blend of features that illustrates the inventiveness of the Vijayanagar courtly style at its best.' He however disagrees with the common belief that this was a queen's residence and thinks it was the king's council chamber.

Wander inside the stark and empty spaces and imagine what it must have been like during the time of Krishnadeva Raya when may be Queen Tirumale Devi lived here – the walls and stucco decorations painted in brilliant colours, the curtains of silk embroidered with seed pearls hanging between the arches and the screens of bamboo at the outer doors; the floors covered in carpets and rugs, the low divans strewn with bolsters; flowers everywhere, garlands swaying over the doorways, incense smoking up from bowls; at dusk, tall brass lamps would be lit to fill the interiors with a mellow golden light and through it all the bejewelled women wandering around with the tinkle of bangles and anklets, waiting for the arrival of the king.

There is a large, three-tiered basement of a palace before the Lotus Mahal which must have been a much larger building. It is one of the largest palace plinths in the Royal Enclosure at 45.7 metres by 28.6 metres and a deep rectangular water tank stands beside it. There is also a long and rather roughly built oblong building in the north-west corner of the *zenana* area that is called the Women's Guard's Quarters but historians can't really agree about the purpose of the mysterious, rather gloomy building. It has just one entrance, no windows, only narrow ventilation slits high up on the walls and a very low, arched ceiling. Some historians think it may have been a storehouse or rather imaginatively a gymnasium for noblemen and not the living quarters for female guards. The watchtowers also have a blend of Hindu and Islamic architectural motifs and according to Michell, there are 'temple-like eaves and towers in combination with Sultanate-style pointed arches and interior domes'. Longhurst imagines these not as watchtowers but as 'pleasure resorts where the royal women could sit without being observed to enjoy the cool breeze', a bit like Jaipur's Hawa Mahal!

Elephant Stables and Guard's Quarters...

Leaving the *zenana* and moving in the opposite direction one comes upon an expansive open space with two large rectangular buildings. Both are built all in stone in a mix of Hindu and Islamic styles and are in surprisingly good condition. One is the Elephant Stables and the other the Guard's Quarters.

The Elephant Stables is a long, narrow structure with a single row of eleven square stalls, each large enough to accommodate two

Previous page: *One of the watchtowers that still stands at a corner of the* zenana *area.*

elephants. Each stall has a high arched door and a domed ceiling and on the roof are a row of nine domes. These domes are in different designs, some circular, others pyramidal with the central one built like a turret with small windows. This may have been where drummers and musicians sat when a military parade was held in the quadrangle in front. Without any of the typical florid touches seen around Hampi, the whole effect is very Islamic in its simplicity and symmetry. One wonders if this rather elaborate building could really have been built to house elephants as there are no iron rings embedded into the floor or walls to hold the animals. Elephants were very important for a martial empire and Abdur Razzaq does write that elephants were tied to the top of the roof with chains.

Unlike the airy structures of Hampi, the oblong Guard's Quarters that stand across from the Elephant Stables has an oddly grim ambience.

At a right angle to the Elephant Stables, across from the open area that could have been a parade ground is another narrow, oblong building with a pillared veranda with pointed arches in front that is called the Guard's Quarters. Inside this rather dark, Gothic-looking building there is an open courtyard surrounded by a covered corridor that Michell speculates may have been used for wrestling matches or the practice of martial arts. It is rather a grim looking building compared to the airy insouciance of the Lotus Mahal and may have been the quarters of soldiers. It does look similar to the Women's Guard's Quarters in the *zenana* courtyard.

The Queen's Bath has a plain, unadorned exterior while the interior is full of lively touches like these arched alcoves.

Pages 242–43: *The Elephant Stables housed the royal elephants in a luxury the common people of the city did not know.*

Queen's Bath and Other Pools...

By the side of the road that connects Kamalapuram village to the royal citadel there is a square rather non-descriptive looking building, surrounded by a moat. Do not be put off by the unprepossessing exterior because it hides a magical world inside.

The outside walls may be unadorned but as you enter through the arched doorway you are in a medieval world of royal pleasure and play. This is the Queen's Bath that has a square pool in the centre surrounded by a broad ornamental corridor with balconies projecting outward above the pool. Along the sides, the wall is pierced by screens so that the light falls on the floor in a dappled carpet of golden light and shadows. There are seats in niches and the ceiling is decorated in stucco patterns. It is feminine and playful and one can imagine the women getting their beauty treatment here – combing their hair, getting an oil massage, crimping and plucking, then diving into the cool waters of the pool; the air filled with laughter and chatter, redolent with perfumes.

Nearby is an octagonal bath with a pillared corridor around it and a fountain in the middle which is in contrast to the Queen's Bath positively Spartan in its masculine layout. There are no stucco designs, arcaded corridors or latticed windows, just grey granite pillars for the bath of warriors and kings. The collapsed stones of an aqueduct lie nearby and show how water was provided to these pools. Nearby there is a 16th-century-temple, the Chandrashekhara Temple dedicated to Shiva and a smaller shrine perched on a hillock to Tiruvengalanatha.

The Bhojanashala *has an intriguing row of stone serving plates used for communal meals.*

BHOJANASHALA...

There is also a small octagonal fountain along the same road and near it rather an intriguing sight awaits visitors. In the middle of a bramble covered field a deep channel has been cut out and lined in granite, with rows of stone slabs placed on both sides. Each slab has a large indented circle like a plate and smaller circles like bowls, 'as if for an outdoor picnic spot for courtiers', as observed by Longhurst. It looks like the site of public feasts with the food being served in stone plates. It is called the *Bhojanashala* which means food hall and tradition says people were fed here and a water channel ran in the middle. There is also a huge stone trough lying nearby carved from a single stone which, according to Longhurst, 'is said to have been kept full of milk for distribution to the poor during the big festivals'.

The 'Underground' Virupaksha Temple...

The 'Underground' Virupaksha Temple, often filled with water, has a giant Shivalingam *in its sanctum.*

This temple stands at the entrance to the royal zone and is still referred to as an underground one as it got completely buried and was excavated by archaeologists. Now because it stands slightly below ground level the interior is often flooded with water and it is rather dark and a depressing sight. The sanctum is empty but inscriptions say it was dedicated to Lord Virupaksha, so probably the *Shivalingam* would have stood in water, like the shrine near the Narasimha statue.

The temple, the only one with the Hazara Rama in the Royal Enclosure stands west of the open quadrangle that is called the Danaik Enclosure. The temple is very simply designed, without elaborate pillars or a decorative *gopuram* and there are many naga stones with carvings of intertwined snakes nearby. In some ways it resembles the simpler designs of the temples one sees on Hemkuta Hill. A stone slab has an inscription that records a grant made by Krishnadeva to Lord Prasanna Virupaksha or 'Virupaksha, the delighted deity' but the architectural style seems to indicate that the temple was built in the 14th century.

THE MAHANAVAMI FESTIVAL

The most gorgeous festival in Vijayanagar was the autumn celebrations of Mahanavami. This is the festival that we still celebrate and call Navaratri and Dussara. In Vijayanagar it was transformed into a celebration of the power and prestige of the empire.

Domingo Paes saw the Mahanavami celebrations sometime after AD 1514 when Krishnadeva Raya had defeated the Gajapati of Orissa and reclaimed the fortress of Udayagiri. So the celebrations were even more magnificent. Paes' detailed, admiring description remains the best account of the parade and religious rituals that took place around the Mahanavami Dibba. Paes went in the entourage of the Portuguese ambassador Christovao de Figueiredo and so he must have been given the front row seat as an honoured guest of Vijayanagar. The trading alliance between Vijayanagar and the Portuguese colony of Goa was crucial for the regular supply of horses that the militant kingdom needed.

Paes describes entering the main palace enclosure where entry was restricted only to the invitees. He writes, 'At the gate are many doorkeepers with leather scourges in their hands, and sticks, and they let no one enter but the captains and chief people.' Once he had entered he noticed, 'Against the gates there were two circles in which were the dancing women richly arrayed with many jewels of gold and diamonds and many pearls.' Inside were the palaces that were built on the stone platforms that we can see today. Here Paes is probably describing the Mahanavami Dibba,

> *This house is called the House of Victory as it was made when the king came back from the war against Orya. . . on the right side of the open space were some narrow scaffoldings made of wood and so lofty that they could be seen over the top of the wall; they were covered at the top with crimson and green velvet and other handsome cloths, and adorned from top to bottom.*

Paes then describes Krishnadeva entering a shrine with Brahman priests to perform puja, where, 'he throws into the fire a powder made up of many things, namely rubies and pearls and all other kinds of precious stones and aloes and other sweet scented things'. Then he comes out into the festival area where the royal horses and elephants stand,

With him a Brahman who takes in his hand a basket full of white roses and approaches the king on the platform, and the king takes three handfuls of these roses, throws them to the horses and after he has thrown them he takes a basket of perfumes and acts towards them as though he would cense them; and when he has finished doing this he reaches towards the elephants and does the same to them.

Once the king is seated on his gold throne the military parade begins,

The captains of the troops approach with shields and spears, and afterwards the captains of the archers; these officers are all stationed on the ground around the arena in front of the elephants, and they constitute the king's guard... As soon as these soldiers have all taken their places the women begin to dance.

Next he describes what seem to be bands of folk dancers, the wrestling matches and fireworks. Then the decorated chariots go past followed by the most important regiment of the army, the cavalry. The horses were:

covered with trappings and cloths of very fine stuff of the king's colours, and with many roses and flowers on their heads and necks, and with their bridles all gilded; and in front of these horses goes a horse with two state umbrellas of the king, and with grander decorations than the others, and one of the lesser equerries leads it by the bridle.

Paes then goes on to describe the ceremonial uniform of the cavalry,

The horsemen were dressed in quilted tunics, also of brocade and velvet and every kind of silk. These tunics are made of layers of very strong raw leather and furnished with iron plates that make them strong; some have these plates gilded both inside and out, and some are made of silver. Their head pieces are in the manner of helmets with borders covering the neck, and each has its piece to protect the face... at the waist they have swords and small battle axes, and in their hands javelins with the shaft covered with gold and silver.

Then came the caparisoned elephants with velvet cloths fringed with gold and bells hanging from their backs. The foot soldiers were so numerous that their battalions stretched as far as the eye could see all wearing uniforms embroidered in gold, carrying swords and shields or bows and arrows, with daggers and battle axes swinging from their waists. He also writes about the 'Moors', the Muslim soldiers with swords, javelins and 'Turkish bows' and men holding muskets.

He was clearly bowled over by the beauty of the royal women,

There come thirty-six of the most beautiful of the king's wives covered with gold and pearls, and much work of seed pearls and in the hands of each a vessel of gold with a lamp of oil burning in it; and with these women came all the female servants and the other wives of the king, with canes in their hands, tipped with gold and with torches burning... these women are so richly bedecked with gold and precious stones that they are hardly able to move.

Fernao Nuniz, who visited Vijayanagar during the reign of Achyuta Raya has also left his account of the Mahanavami celebrations and describes rather an intriguing ritual during the king's review of the troops.

At the end he dismounts and takes a bow in his hand and shoots three arrows, namely one for the Ydallcao (Sultan Adil Shah of Bijapur) and another for the King of Cotamuloco (sultan of Golconda) and yet another for the Portuguese.

The final words on the Mahanavami festival belong to Paes, totally overwhelmed by what he saw, 'I have no words to express what I saw... with my head so often turned from one side to the other that I was almost falling backwards off my horse with my senses lost'.

An exquisite carving of a dancing girl in green chlorite.

Chronology

1336 – foundation of the kingdom of Vijayanagar; accession of Harihara I
1340 – Bukka conquers Penugonda
1342 – death of Hoysala king Vira Ballala III
1346 – Bukka conquers Hoysala kingdom
1352 – Kumara Kampana captures Ma'abar
1356 – accession of Bukka I
1360 – Tamil areas conquered
1374 – death of Kumara Kampana
1377 – accession of Harihara II
1380 – Goa and Konkan annexed
1398 – Vijayanagar invaded by Bahmani forces
1404 – accession of Virupaksha
1405 – accession of Bukka II
1406 – accession of Deva Raya I
1419 – Deva Raya I defeats Firuz Bahmani
1424 – accession of Deva Raya II
1428 – Deva Raya II captures Kondavidu
1443 – Deva Raya II invades Bahmani kingdom
1446 – death of Deva Raya II
1446– 65 – various minor kings
1469 – rise of Saluva Narasimha
1485 – accession of Saluva Narasimha
1490 – Narasa Nayaka as regent
1503 – accession of Vira Narasimha
1509 – accession of Krishnadeva Raya
1509 – defeats the Bahmani kingdom
1512 – capture of Raichur Fort
1513 – capture of Udayagiri Fort
1520 – defeats the kingdom of Bijapur
1529 – accession of Achyuta Raya
1543 – accessions of Venkata I / Tirumala I
1544 – joint rule of Sadashiva and Rama Raya
1565 – Battle of Talikota; Vijayanagar abandoned

Further Reading

Aiyangar, S. Krishnaswamy, ed. *Vijayanagar, History and Legacy*. Monograph. University of Mysore. 1936.

Basham, A. L. *Wonder That Was India*. London: Sidgewick & Jackson. 1956.

Brown, Percy. *Indian Architecture*. Mumbai: Taraporevala. 1955.

Devakunjari, D. *Hampi*. New Delhi: Archaeological Survey of India. 1992.

Fergusson, J. *History of Indian and Eastern Architecture*. London: John Murray. 1910.

Filliozat, Vasundhara. *Vijayanagar*. New Delhi: National Book Trust. 1977.

Fritz, John M. and George Michell. *Hampi*. Mumbai: India Book House. 2003.

Greenlaw, Alexander and John Gollings. *Vijayanagar*. Mysore: Government of Karnataka. 1988.

Longhurst, A. H. *Hampi Ruins*. Delhi: Asian Educational Services. 1917 (first published).

Majumdar, R. C., ed. *The History and Culture of the Indian People*. Delhi: Bharatiya Vidya Bhawan.

Michell, George. *The Vijayanagar Courtly Style*. Delhi: Manohar. 1992.

Sastri, Nilakanta. *History of South India*. Delhi: Oxford University Press. 1955.

Satyan, T. S. and S. Srinivasachar. *Hampi*. Mysore: Karnataka Tourism Department. 1995.

Sen Gupta, Subhadra. *Great Temples of India*. Delhi: Rupa. 2001.

Sewell, Robert. *Forgotten Empire*. Delhi: Asian Educational Services. 1900 (first published).

Stein, Burton. *Vijayanagar*. Delhi: Cambridge University Press. 1993.

Verghese, Anila. *Monumental Legacy, Hampi*. Delhi: Oxford University Press. 2002.

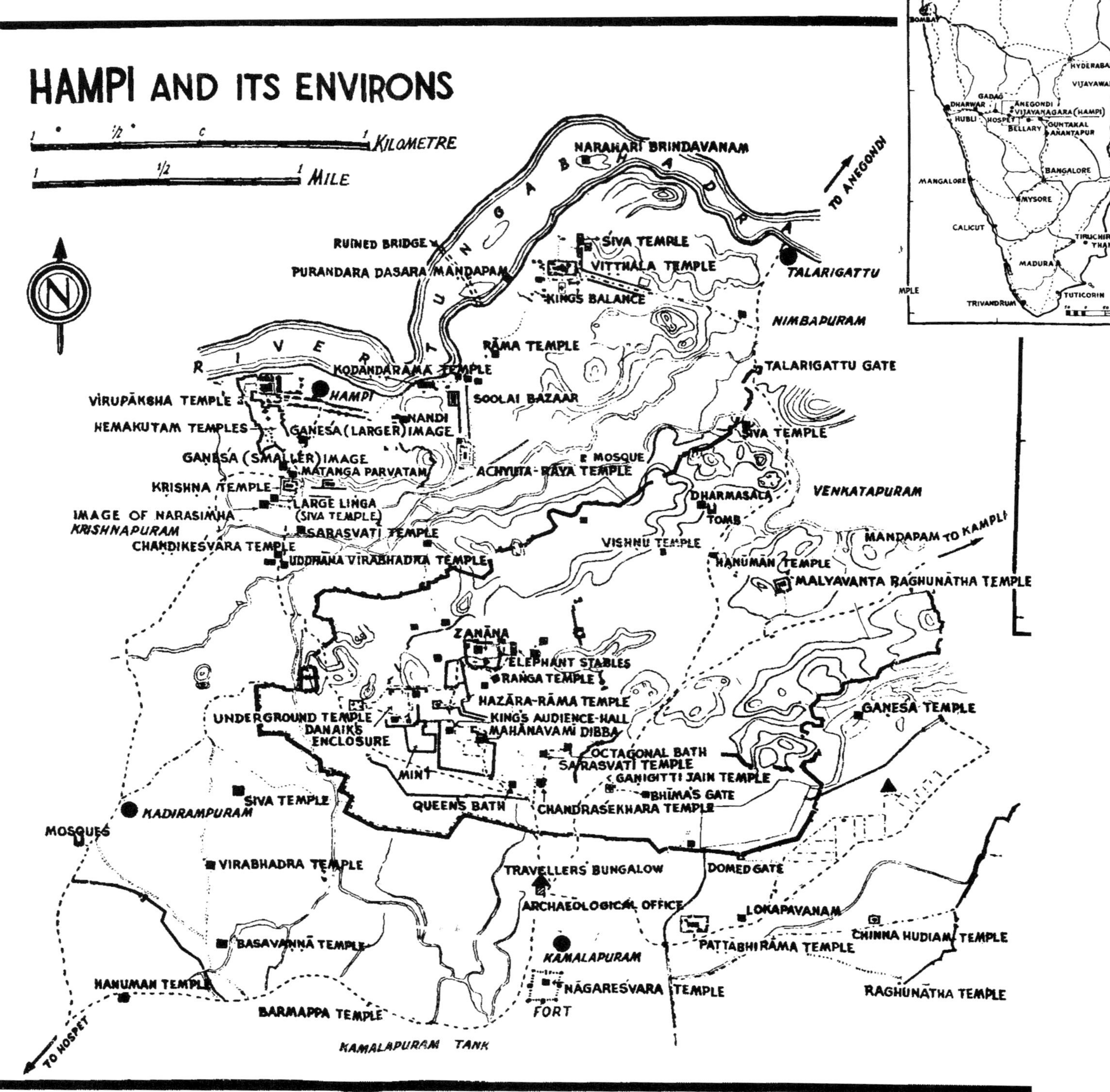

HAMPI AND ITS ENVIRONS
KILOMETRE
MILE
N
RIVER TUNGABHADRA
TO ANEGONDI
NARAHARI BRINDAVANAM
RUINED BRIDGE
SIVA TEMPLE
PURANDARA DASARA MANDAPAM
VITTHALA TEMPLE
TALARIGATTU
KINGS BALANCE
NIMBAPURAM
RĀMA TEMPLE
TALARIGATTU GATE
KODANDARAMA TEMPLE
VIRUPĀKSHA TEMPLE
HAMPI
SOOLAI BAZAAR
NANDI IMAGE
HEMAKUTAM TEMPLES
GANESA (LARGER) IMAGE
SIVA TEMPLE
GANESA (SMALLER) IMAGE
MOSQUE
MATANGA PARVATAM
ACHYUTA-RAYA TEMPLE
KRISHNA TEMPLE
VENKATAPURAM
DHARMASALA
LARGE LINGA (SIVA TEMPLE)
IMAGE OF NARASIMHA
TOMB
KRISHNAPURAM
SARASVATI TEMPLE
MANDAPAM TO KAMPLI
CHANDIKESVARA TEMPLE
VISHNU TEMPLE
UDDHANA VIRABHADRA TEMPLE
HANUMAN TEMPLE
MALYAVANTA RAGHUNATHA TEMPLE
ZANĀNA
ELEPHANT STABLES
RANGA TEMPLE
HAZĀRA-RĀMA TEMPLE
GANESA TEMPLE
UNDERGROUND TEMPLE
KINGS AUDIENCE-HALL
DANAIKS ENCLOSURE
MAHĀNAVAMI DIBBA
OCTAGONAL BATH
SARASVATI TEMPLE
MINT
GANIGITTI JAIN TEMPLE
BHIMAS GATE
SIVA TEMPLE
QUEENS BATH
CHANDRASEKHARA TEMPLE
KADIRAMPURAM
MOSQUES
VIRABHADRA TEMPLE
TRAVELLERS BUNGALOW
DOMED GATE
ARCHAEOLOGICAL OFFICE
LOKAPAVANAM
BASAVANNĀ TEMPLE
PATTABHIRĀMA TEMPLE
CHINNA HUDIAM TEMPLE
KAMALAPURAM
HANUMAN TEMPLE
NĀGARESVARA TEMPLE
RAGHUNATHA TEMPLE
BARMAPPA TEMPLE
FORT
KAMALAPURAM TANK
TO HOSPET
BOMBAY
HYDERABAD
VIJAYAWADA
GADAG
DHARWAR
ANEGONDI
VIJAYANAGARA (HAMPI)
HUBLI
HOSPET
GUNTAKAL
BELLARY
ANANTAPUR
BANGALORE
MANGALORE
MADRAS
MYSORE
CALICUT
TIRUCHIRAPPALLI
THANJAVUR
MADURAI
TUTICORIN
TRIVANDRUM
MILES

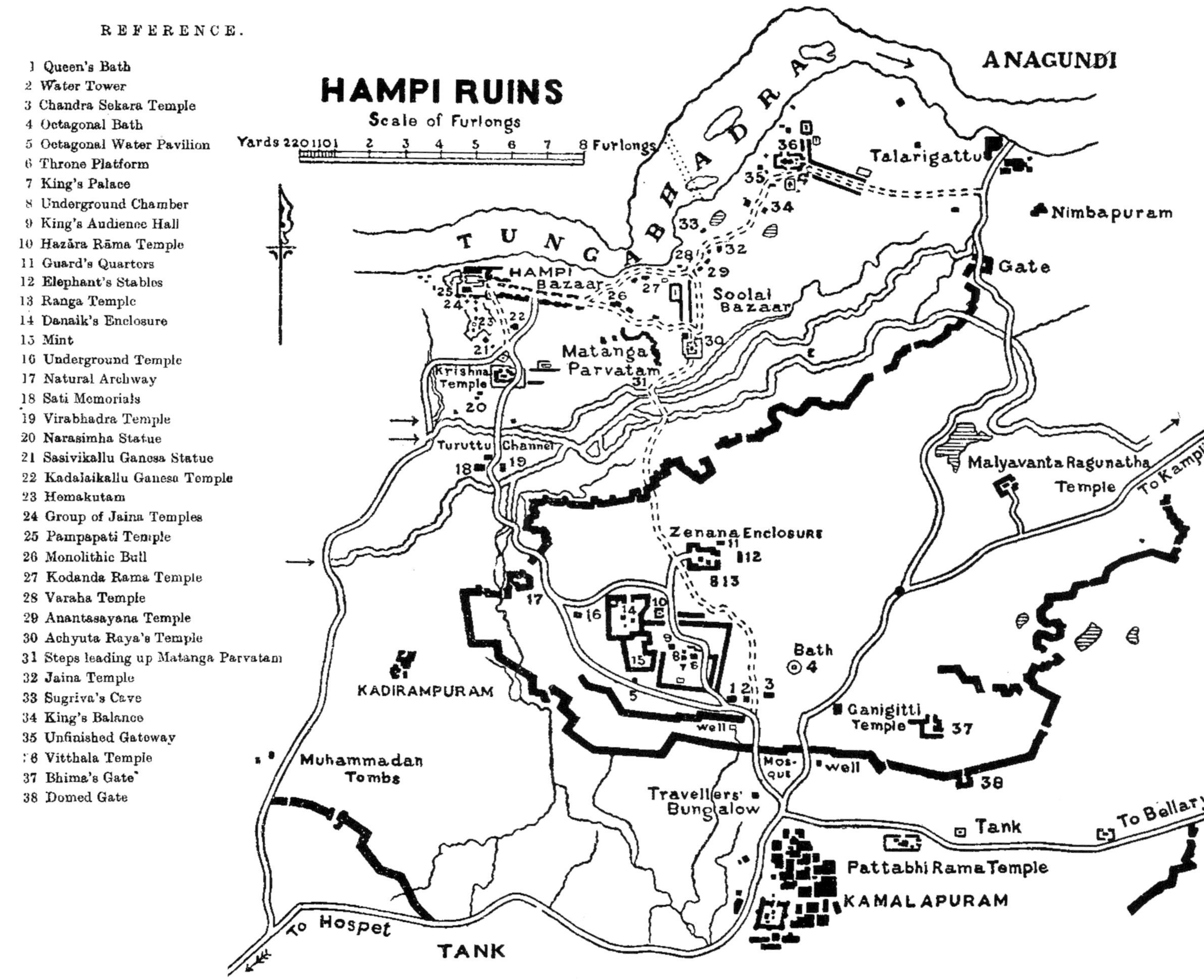
REFERENCE.
1 Queen's Bath
2 Water Tower
3 Chandra Sekara Temple
4 Octagonal Bath
5 Octagonal Water Pavilion
6 Throne Platform
7 King's Palace
8 Underground Chamber
9 King's Audience Hall
10 Hazāra Rāma Temple
11 Guard's Quarters
12 Elephant's Stables
13 Ranga Temple
14 Danaik's Enclosure
15 Mint
16 Underground Temple
17 Natural Archway
18 Sati Memorials
19 Virabhadra Temple
20 Narasimha Statue
21 Sasivikallu Ganesa Statue
22 Kadalaikallu Ganesa Temple
23 Hemakutam
24 Group of Jaina Temples
25 Pampapati Temple
26 Monolithic Bull
27 Kodanda Rama Temple
28 Varaha Temple
29 Anantasayana Temple
30 Achyuta Raya's Temple
31 Steps leading up Matanga Parvatam
32 Jaina Temple
33 Sugriva's Cave
34 King's Balance
35 Unfinished Gateway
36 Vitthala Temple
37 Bhima's Gate
38 Domed Gate
HAMPI RUINS
Scale of Furlongs
Yards 220 110 1 2 3 4 5 6 7 8 Furlongs
ANAGUNDI
TUNGABHADRA
Talarigattu
Nimbapuram
Gate
HAMPI Bazaar
Soolai Bazaar
Matanga Parvatam
Krishna Temple
Turuttu Channel
Malyavanta Ragunatha Temple
To Kampli
Zenana Enclosure
Bath
Ganigitti Temple
KADIRAMPURAM
Muhammadan Tombs
well
Mosque
Travellers' Bungalow
Tank
To Bellary
Pattabhi Rama Temple
KAMALAPURAM
To Hospet
TANK

Index

A

Achyuta Raya (1529–42), 87, 99, 100, 104, 129, 143, 182, 186–90, 196, 225, 250

Adil Shah, Sultan of Bijapur, 250

Advaita, 62, 68, 69

Agraharas, 62

Ahmednagar, 92, 101, 104

Akbar, 8, 10, 103, 104, 113, 117

Akka Mahadevi, 169

Akkadevi, Chalukyan princess, 151

Allauddin Khalji. *See* Khalji Dynasty

Amukta Malyada, 118

Anantasayana Vishnu, 29

Anantashayanagudi, 223

Anegondi, 54, 55, 56, 59, 219, 222

Anjaneya, 144

Anjenadri, 21, 26, 36

antarala, 168

Apsaras and *Yakshis*, 27–30

Arab traders, 65, 82, 90, 130, 133, 231

Aravidu Dynasty, 103

architecture and sculpture, 10–12, 27, 117, 161–64, 217*ff*

Ashoka, 26

Ashtadiggajas, 117

B

Babur, 104

Badrinath, 68

Bahmani Dynasty, 13, 62, 75, 76, 78–80, 90, 92, 93, 104, 105–06, 222

Firuz, 78–81, 83, 105–07

Mahmud Shah, 90, 92–93

Balagopal, 192

Ballalla III, 59

Bankapur Fort, 107

Barbosa, Duarte, 32, 33, 144, 146–48

Basavanna, 169, 172

Basham, A L, 161–63

Bay of Bengal, 60

Bellary, 26, 51

Belur Temple, 49

Berar, 92, 101, 104

Bhakti saints, 169

Bharatnatyam, 155

Bhatkal, 140

Bhima, 224

Bhojanashala in Royal Enclosure, 245

Bhuvaneshwari, 28, 173, 181

Bidar, 92, 93, 101, 104, 113

Bidjanagar, 17, 131

Bijapur, 92, 98, 100, 101, 104, 113

Birbal, Raja, 117

Bisnaga, 17, 31–33, 36

Brahmanical heritage, 45

Brahmotsavam festival, 21, 29, 32, 42, 139

Brihadishwara Temple, 154

Brihat Samhita, 161

Brown, Percy, 160, 170, 210, 229–30

Buddha, 45

Bukka I (1356–77), 27, 36, 56, 59–60, 62–65, 68, 69, 73, 75–79, 104, 160, 184
Bukka II (1405–6), 104, 198

C

Calicut, 140
caste divisions, 148–49
Chalukyas, 26, 151, 164, 182
Chandragiri, 36
Chaul, 78
Cheng Ho, 133
Chettiyars, 146
Chidambaram, 69, 140, 164
China and India, trade, 133
Chinna Devi, queen of Vijayanagar, 95, 98, 122
Chitragni Mahal. *See* Lotus Mahal
Cholamandalam, 36
colonial powers, 103
craftsmen and merchants of Vijayanagar, 144–46

D

Dabhol, 78
Danaik Enclosure and the Mint in Royal Enclosure, 235, 236–37, 247
Dandanayaka, Timma, 98–99
dei Conti, Nicolo, 31, 32, 79
Delhi Sultanate, 27, 43–44, 54, 56, 76, 222
Deva Raya I (1406–22), 31, 2, 75, 79–84, 104, 105–07, 143, 225
Deva Raya II (1424–46), 31, 75, 84–85, 104, 176, 205, 221
devadasis, 28, 33, 137, 151, 152, 154–55, 169
Devagiri (Daulatabad), 51, 55
Devakunjari, D, 164, 203, 208, 223, 238
Dharwar, 51
Dravidian architecture, 27, 208
Durga, 180, 181
Dvarasamudra, 49, 50
Dwarka, Gujarat, 68

E

Ekambaranatha temples, 164
Elephant Stables and Guard's Quarters in Royal Enclosure, 72, 240–41, 242–43, 244
Ellamma, 144

F

Fatehpur Sikri, 8, 10, 113
Federici, Ceasaro, 31
Fergusson, James, 157
Ferishta, Mohammad Qasim, 80, 105–07;
Tarikh-i-Firishta, 105–07
Figueiredo, Christovao de, 97–98, 122, 248
Firozshah. *See* Bahmani Dynasty
fortifications in Royal Enclosure, 221–24
Fritz, John M., 126

G

Gajapati kings of Kalinga, 49,50, 76, 81, 83, 92, 94, 96–97, 192, 231, 248
Prataparudra, 92, 94, 97, 124
Ganagitti Jain Temple, 196, 198, 198–99
Ganesha, 184, 185–87, 211
Ganga Devi, 77, 149
garbha grihas, 28, 34, 64, 165, 168, 187
Garshasp Malik. *See* Khalji, Allauddin
Gingee, 103
Goa, 77, 78, 82
Golconda, 92, 97, 100, 101, 104, 250
gopurams, 7, 9, 11, 19, 29, 46–47, 48, 52–53, 74, 111, 115, 116–17, 138, 139, 160, 161, 164, 171, 205
Gulbarga, 75, 93, 107, 113, 222

H

Halebid Temple, 49
Hampi Bazaar, 9, 11, 21, 48, 64, 117, 129, 133, 144, 147, 159, 173, 176, 181–82, 182, 185, 187, 189, 191, 192, 205, 219

Hampi, revived, 34–35. *See* also Vijayanagar
Hanuman, 23, 44, 144, 150, 191, 192, 198
Harihara I (1336–56), 27, 36, 56, 59–60, 62–65, 68, 69, 73, 75, 104, 160, 184
Harihara II (1377–1404), 78, 104
Hasan Khan, son of Firuz Shah Bahmani, 107
Hazara Rama Temple, 23, 116, 135, 144, 224–25, 224, 226–27, 228, 247
  kalyana mandapa, 225, 228
Hemkuta Hill, 9, 21, 129, 159, 182; temples, 55, 61, 173, 174–75, 183–85
Hiranyakasipu, 195
Hiriya Tirumalaraja, 189
Honawar, 140
Hospet, Bellary, 20, 172, 222
Hoysalas, 26, 49, 50, 59–60, 65, 164
  Vir Ballala, 50

I
Ibn Batuta, 151
Indian Ocean, 60, 133
irrigation systems, 116
Irugappa, 198
Islam, 44, 45, 54, 56
Ismail Adil Khan, 97, 98

J
Jaganmohini. *See* Tuka
Jahangir, 105
Jain Temples, 65
Jinanatha, Kunthu, 198
Joshimath, Uttarakhand, 68

K
Kadirampuram, 223
Kafur, Malik, 49, 50, 51, 54, 68
Kakatiya, kings of Warangal, 49, 50, 54
  Prataparudra I, 49–50
Kali, 144
Kamakoti Peetha, Kanchipuram, 68
Kamalapuram, 34, 129, 223, 244
Kambham, 125
Kampana Kumara, 62, 77, 149
Kampiladeva, 55–56, 184, 219
Kampili, 26, 51, 54–56, 57, 68, 198, 222
Kanchipuram, 140
Kapilar, Sangam poet, 143
Kapiyanar, Kappiyaru, 111–12
Kara, 41–42
Khalji Dynasty, 41–44, 49, 51, 54
  Allauddin Khalji, 27, 41–44, 49, 50, 51, 54
  Jalaluddin Khalji, 41–42
Khusro, Amir, 50
Kichaka, 224
Kishkindha, 17, 21, 23, 192
Kodandarama Temple, 23, 189, 191–92;
  deepa stambha, 191
Kondavidu Fort, 94–96
Kotalingam, 12
Kovelakonda Battle, 93
Kramrisch, Stella, 162
Krishna, Lord, 17, 60, 65, 76, 81, 84, 165, 182, 192, 211
Krishna Temple, 182, 192–95;
gopuram, 192, 193
Krishnabhatta, 195
Krishnadeva Raya (1509–29), 8, 21, 31, 48, 76, 87, 90, 92–99, 100, 104, 109*ff*, 124–25, 131, 137, 142–43, 176–77, 189, 192, 193, 195, 205, 212, 215, 225, 228, 231, 239, 248–49;
  army and cavalry, 249–50;
  titles—*Andhra Bhoja* (King of the Andhras), *Kannada Rajya Rama Ramana* (Great King of the Kannadas) and *Moorurayaraganda* (King of Three Seas), 118
Krishnaswamy Temple, Vijayanagar, 95, 115, 171

L
Lakshman, 23, 192, 198, 224, 228
Lakshmi, 170, 196, 211, 228
Lodi Dynasty, 104

Longhurst, A H, 217, 238, 240
Lopes, Senhor David, 31
Lotus Mahal, 11, 13, 30, 115–16, 134, 238–40, 238, 244. *See also* Royal Enclosure

M

Madhavacharya. *See* Vidyaranya
Madhura Vijayam, 77, 149
Madurai, 69, 140, 164
Mahabharata, 8, 224
Mahanavami festival, 33, 98, 137, 151, 155, 216–17, 230–31, 248–50
Mahanavami platform in Royal Enclosure, 9, 12, 13, 152, 216–17, 228–35, 232, 248–50.
Mahishasuramardini, 181
Mahmud of Ghazni, 45
Mahmud Shah *See* Bahmani Dynasty
Malabar Coast, 146
Malayavanta Raghunatha Temple, 198
Malayavanta Hill, 21, 23, 225
Malik Mohammad, 56
Malika Jahan, 41–43
Mallikarjuna (1446–65), 104
Malpannagudi, 223
Malwa, invasion by Allauddin Khalji, 42
mandapas, 28, 64, 115, 119, 160, 164, 168, 178, 187, 196
Mangalore, 77, 140
Marappa, 62
Matanga Hill, 9, 11, 21, 23, 48, 129, 173, 182, 182, 187
Maurya Dynasty, 26
Meenakshi, the Goddess of Madura, 77
Michell, George, 18, 126, 135, 238, 239–40, 244
Ming Dynasty, 75, 133
Mudappa, 62
Mudgal, 100
Mudkul, 105–07
Mughal Empire, 8, 103, 104
Muhammad I, 76
Muhammad of Ghur, 49
Mujahid, 76
Mukhalingam, 180, 185
Muslims, 146, 220, 250
Mylapur, 140

N

Nagalapura, 116, 123
Nagambika, 123
Naib, Malik, 36
Nalanda, 45
Nandi, 12, 129, 198, 211
Narasimha (deity), 9, 144, 172, 194, 195–96, 228
Narasimha II (1491–1505), 104
natya mandapa, 140, 169
Nayaka kings, 164, 103
Narasa Nayaka (1491–1503), 86–87, 90, 104
Nayaka, Singiya, 51
Nellore, 77
Nikitin, Athanasius, 32
Nizam-ul-Mulk, 36
Nuniz, Fernao, 31–32, 35, 82,124, 151, 230, 250

O

octagonal Bath, 221

P

Paes, Domingo, 31–33, 35, 82, 98, 118–19, 122–23, 137, 147, 151, 155, 221, 230, 231, 248–49, 250
Pampa, Goddess, 9, 20–21, 28, 64, 83, 127, 139, 143, 149, 173, 178, 181, 191, 225
Pandharpur, 208
Pandyas of Malabar, 49, 50, 54, 164
Panipat, Battle (1526), 104
Pampakshetra, 17, 21, 31
Parvati, 143, 159, 170
Pattabhirama Temple, 96, 169, 170
Pedanna, Allasani, 117
Penugonda Fort, 90, 103
Pertal, 105–07
Pires, Tome, 32

Portuguese, 100, 103, 115, 116, 130, 133
Prabuddha Deva Raya (1485), 86, 104
pradakshina patha, 28, 165
prakaras, 171, 187
Prasanna Virupaksha, 247
Prataparudra. Gajapati, *See* Gajapati kings of Orissa
Prataparudra I, Kakatiya king. *See* Kakatiya kings of Warangal
Puri, Orissa, 68

Q
Queen's Bath and other pools in Royal Enclosure, 244–45, 244
Quli, Qutub Shah, 97

R
Raghavacharlu, K, 109
Raghunatha, 151
Raghunatha, Lord, 77
Raichur Doab, 76, 80, 93
Raichur, 51, 97, 100;
  Fort, siege of, 122
Raja Raja Chola, 154
Rajamundry, 97
Rakkasige, 101
Rakshasi-Tangadi Battle, 101
Ram, 23, 150, 165, 192, 198, 211, 224
Rama Raya, 100–01, 123, 151
Ramabhadramba, wife of Raghunatha, 151
Ramachandra (1422), 83
Ramachandra Deva, Raja of Devagiri (d.1312 AD), 43, 51, 104
Ramalingeshwara, 185
Ramayana, 21, 23, 158, 178, 191, 192, 200–01, 225
Rameshwaram, 50, 69
Ranthambhor, 49
Rashtrakutas, 26
Razzaq, Abdur, 31, 131, 140, 142, 221–23, 234, 235, 241
Reddis of Rajamundry, 76, 80, 106
Royal Enclosure, 11. *See also* Hazara Rama Temple
royal life, 134–40

S
Sadashiva, Tuluva king. *See* Tuluva Dynasty
Salim Chishti, Sheikh, 10
Saluva Dynasty, 86–87, 104
  Narasimha (1485–91), 86, 90, 104
  Timma, 92, 95, 97, 98–99, 122, 125
Sangama Dynasty, 39, 51, 56, 58–59, 62, 65, 73, 75–85, 86, 104
Saraswati, 211
Sarnath, 45
Sastri, Nilakanta, 50, 65, 71, 149
Sayana, 68, 69, 79
Sayyid Dynasty, 104
Seringapattanam, 123
Sewell, Robert, 14, 31, 35, 54, 60, 79, 102
Shahrukh, Sultan of Persia, 31, 131
Shaiva shrines, 160, 184
Shankara Deva, 51
Shankaracharya, 56, 68, 69
Sharada Peetha Math of Sringeri, 27, 58–59, 62, 65, 68, 69
Sharada, Goddess, 62
Shilpa Shastra, 162
Shitab Khan, 97
Shiva Dakshinamurti, 165
Shiva, 9, 21, 64, 68, 83, 143, 169, 170, 173, 178
Shivalingam, 27, 180, 184, 195, 198, 223, 247
Shrikantaya, S, 62
Simhachalam, 97
Sita, 23, 198, 211, 224
Southern kingdoms, 49–56
Srirangam, 69, 77, 164
Srisailam, 140
sthalapurana, 21
Subramanian, P, 154
Subramanya, Lord, 195
Sugriva, 21, 23, 192
Surya worship, 127
symbolism, 62

T

Telarigattu Ghat, 73, 219
Talikota Battle, 31, 100–1, 208, 220
Tangadi, 101
Taxila, 45
temples on Hemkuta Hill, 183–85
Tenali Ramakrishna Kavi, 117
Thanjavur, 103
Thimma Bhupala (1491), 104
Timur, 31, 45, 60
Tirumalamba Devi, wife of Rama Raya, 123, 151
Tirumale Devi, queen of Vijayanagar, 95, 98, 122–23, 239
Tirupati shrine. *See* Venkateshwara Temple
Tiruvengalanatha Temple, 129, 143, 182, 187, 188–89
Tripurari, 178
Tughlak Dynasty, 44, 51, 55, 56, 68, 69, 104
  Ferozshah, 60
  Ghiyasuddin, 54
  Muhammad bin, 27, 36, 54–56, 60
Tuka (Jaganmohini), 123, 124–25
Tulapurusha-dana ritual, 215
Tuluva Dynasty, 87, 90–92, 102, 104, 111
  Sadashiva (1542–70), 102, 104
Tungabhadra, 9, 11, 12, 13, 16, 17, 19, 20, 21, 26, 41, 51, 54, 59, 63, 68, 76, 81, 93, 126–27, 130, 131, 138, 156, 157, 158, 159*ff*, 189, 191, 215

U

Udayagiri, 36, 86, 94–95, 116, 124, 192–93
Underground temple in Royal Enclosure, 246–47
untouchables, 149

V

Vaishnava temples, 160, 228
Valli, 21, 23, 192
Varadaraja, 164
Varadevi, queen of Achyuta Raya, 196
Varaha, 64
Varthema, Ludovico di, 31, 137
Vastupurusha Mandala, 27, 161
Vedas, 68, 79
Velamas of Telengana, 76, 106
Vengalamba, 123
Vengi, 97
Venkataramanayya, N, 78
Venkateshwara-Balaji, Lord, 116, 119, 143
Venkateshwara Temple, Tirupati, 95
Venugopal, Lord, 233
Vidyaranya, 9, 27, 57–60, 62–65, 68, 69, 79, 178, 181, 185
Vidyateertha Muni, 68
Vijaya I (son of Deva Raya I), 83
Vijayanagar Empire, 8;
  defeated by Muslim invaders, 7, 30, 34;
  citizens, 146–49;
  fall of, 102–03;
  history, 71*ff*;
  invasion by Firuz Shah Bahmani, 106–07;
  landscape and panorama, 17–36;
  sunset, 12;
  women and children, 8, 149, 151–52, 154–55;
  before Vijayanagar, 26–27
Vir Ballala. *See* Hoysalas
Vira Narasimha (1503–9), 87, 90, 104
Vira Vijaya Bukka (1422–24), 104
Virabhadra, Prince of Vijayanagar, 96, 124
Virupaksha I (1404–5), 78–79, 104
Virupaksha II (1465–85), 104
Virupaksha Temple, Hampi, 7, 9–10, 21, 28, 32, 35, 50, 52–53, 54, 61, 64, 75, 79, 117, 133, 172, 173–81, 185, 192, 225;
  deepa stambha, 177;
  gopuram, 46–47, 52–53, 74, 133, 138, 139, 147, 159, 159, 173, 176, 182, 183;

mandapa, 177
Virupaksha, Lord, 9, 21, 64, 65, 129, 139, 143, 173, 178, 182, 247
Virupakshapura, 17, 21
Vishnu, 64, 68, 115, 144, 187, 211, 213, 224, 228
Vitthala Lord, 182, 205, 208, 213
Vitthala Temple, 22, 23, 26, 77, 79, 91, 99, 110, 111, 117, 118, 120–21, 123, 143, 160, 164, 168–69, 196, 202–03, 204, 205*ff*, 205, 209, 225;
gopuram, 143;
maha mandapa and *kalyana mandapa*, 206–07, 212, 213;
natya mandapa, 140
Vitthalaswami Temple, 171

W

Warangal, 49, 50, 54

Y

Yadava, Kingdom of Devagiri, 26, 43, 49, 50
Yusuf Adil Khan, ruler of Bijapur, 90, 92–93

Z

zenana in Royal Enclosure, 133, 134, 172, 220, 237–40, 239